BRIAN FRIEL

Essays, Diaries, Interviews

1964–1999

edited, introduced and with a bibliography
by Christopher Murray

faber and faber
LONDON·NEW YORK

This collection first published in 1999
by Faber and Faber Limited
3 Queen Square London WC1N 3AU
Published in the United States by Faber and Faber Inc.,
a division of Farrar, Straus and Giroux Inc., New York

Typeset by Faber and Faber Ltd
Printed in England by Clays Ltd, St Ives plc

A CIP record for this book
is available from the British Library

ISBN 0–571–20069–9

2 4 6 8 10 9 7 5 3 1

Contents

Introduction

This volume is intended to mark Brian Friel's seventieth birthday in 1999. In one way, a book of critical essays might be considered the more appropriate publication to mark the occasion, but in recent years there have been two such volumes, edited by Alan J. Peacock and William Kerwin respectively, and in 1999 two journals plan similar *festschriften*, namely *Irish University Review* and the *Hungarian Journal of English and American Studies*. In addition, there have been full-length books on Friel by (in chronological order) D. E. S. Maxwell, George O'Brien, Ulf Dantanus, Richard Pine and Elmer Andrews. An indication of the steady increase in the publication of essays and articles on Friel is also made plain by George O'Brien's *Brian Friel: A Reference Guide 1962–1992*, published in 1995. No fewer than 800 entries are included here. Thus a volume that takes a different track seems in order. And a volume that gathers together Brian Friel's fugitive pieces and those interviews which, while sometimes going over old ground, contain nuggets of rare information and critical opinion, is something that fills an important gap in Friel studies.

Notoriously, Brian Friel is a shy man, reticent in public and sparing in his comments on his own work to a Beckettian degree. He is not one to intrude and set the record straight for posterity, to act Lombard to the making of his own history. For years the scholars who have written about his work have recognized the value of a number of Friel's occasional essays and interviews, but as these were often first published in obscure and difficult-to-obtain sources it may be thought useful to have these made available now in a convenient format. In addition, there are three pieces never before published: an interview given in 1986 for use in a volume on Education and the Arts edited by the late Dr Daniel Murphy of Trinity College, Dublin, and two further extracts from Friel's sporadic diary, relating to the genesis of

Molly Sweeney (1994) and *Give Me Your Answer, Do!* (1997). As those who have worked on earlier extracts from Friel's diary well know, these records are distilled poems about the writing process itself. Yet in their coded, cryptic style they also reveal to the careful reader a startling amount about the sources of Friel's later plays and their subtexts. In a way, these diary extracts are the key to this whole volume. They tell us that with Brian Friel it is by indirections we find directions out. Like birdwatchers we must wait patiently for the chance to see a habitat, a flash of colour, a hatching. It takes time. There are few soundbites here, few rhetorical flourishes aimed at the shapers of cultural reputations or the setters of examination papers in contemporary drama. But if we approach quietly and open-mindedly, we can share in a major writer's struggle to be himself and to respond to the world around him. It is not a spirit of reverence that is demanded but a spirit of alertness to and of sympathy with the writer's endeavour. In the end, the words he chooses and uses in interview, in essay, and in diary extract lead us back to the texts of the plays themselves with a greater understanding both of their cost in creation and their artistic achievement.

Friel began his writing career as a writer of short stories. He wrote for *The New Yorker* in the late 1950s and early 1960s and two volumes of these stories were published under the titles *A Saucer of Larks* (1962) and *The Gold in the Sea* (1966). They have subsequently been published in various edited collections, as in the *Selected Stories of Brian Friel* (1979), and in *The Diviner and Other Stories* (1983). Friel belongs to a great tradition of Irish story-telling which stretches from William Carleton in the nineteenth century through George Moore and James Joyce in the early twentieth century and Sean O'Faolain, Frank O'Connor, Michael McLaverty and Mary Lavin in the mid-century. It is a form now almost defunct in Ireland, and Friel may well, alongside William Trevor, be one of the last practitioners. For the short story in the Irish tradition was a leisurely, usually rural-bound form, exploratory of character and states of feeling in a world governed by settled seasonal patterns and rituals. The urban stamp imposed by Joyce and given an insolent flourish by Beckett had all but faded when Friel began to publish. By the middle of this century the world of the Irish short story was a world where authority was taken for granted; a patriarchal and religiously conservative society, dependent on mild eccentricity and occasional bouts of passionate revolt for its repertoire of stories. It was a world peopled by well-fed, ruminative priests, schoolteachers sporting immortal longings, copious inadequate fathers, wistful mothers and a seemingly endless succession of adolescent children poised on the threshold of disillusion. Friel appeared to be aware that he was working within an exhausted form. His stories, while set in a rural landscape, are always imbued with a melancholy which marks a persistent sense of dislocation, betrayal and disappointment. Stories such as 'A Saucer of Larks', 'The Potato Gatherers', 'Mr Synge, My Heart's Delight', 'The Diviner' and 'The Foundry House' have a lyrical quality which render experience as essentially precious and intense but also laden with intimations of loss. Indeed, it is in such stories that one first hears that strong Frielian music reminiscent of nothing more than the theme Beckett announced in his precocious little book on Proust in the early 1930s, that the only Paradise worth writing about is 'the Paradise that has been lost'. The vision of life permeating Friel's stories is a tragic one, and in time the short-story form proved too narrow to contain it.

But it is as a playwright that Friel is best known internationally. Hence this book only contains a selection of such pieces – interviews and articles by Friel himself – that relate to the drama. By the time he turned to writing full-time in 1960 Friel had had two radio plays produced by the BBC Northern Ireland Home Service, *A Sort of Freedom* (January 1958) and *To This Hard House* (April 1958). Neither of these has been published. The first is a problem play centred on businessman Jack Frazer, being forced by the trade union to sack a man unwilling to join. Jack at first encourages this man, Joe Reddin, to stand his ground: they have been friends for decades. Parallel with this situation is Frazer's resistance to inoculating a baby he and his wife have adopted. The issue in both plots is the nature of freedom. Here, in a play which tends to be ignored by the critics, is a theme not only central to Friel's work but to the whole Northern political situation as this was going to be explosively exposed ten years later. Frazer is a version of the unscrupulous wielder of power who at first promises to stand by his blindly loyal employee Reddin – 'There are ways and means of getting round problems like that' – and who shifts his ground when it becomes expedient to sack Reddin. Mrs Reddin puts the point very clearly to her husband:

> Rights, rights! That's all I hear these days. You talking about your rights, and your conscience, and now him talking about his rights. I'm all through-other [confused] listening to rights and liberties so that I don't know any more what's right and what's wrong. But one thing I do know, Joe, rights are all very fine when you have money to support them, like Jack Frazer there.

It must be borne in mind that this play dates from two years before Sam Thompson's controversial *Over the Bridge*, the first stage play to put on stage labour differences and sectarianism in modern Northern Ireland. Friel stays away from the sectarian issue, but his radio play, in focusing on freedom of choice and showing its illusory nature, indirectly addresses it.

Equally interesting, however, is the way this play introduces what Mrs Frazer calls the 'withered soul' motif. As will be seen in Friel's interview with Desmond Rushe in this volume, Friel has a particular interest in the desiccation of spirit in late twentieth-century life, in Ireland as elsewhere. In *A Sort of Freedom* Frazer's aggressiveness and lack of humanity are linked with his marriage problems. A sterile marriage is here a metaphor for a sterile materialism. Frazer forced the adoption of a baby on his wife to cover up the loss of identity he was beginning to feel. This is why he feels the baby's death as catastrophic: 'He was called Jack Frazer after me. He would have been me.' But his wife sees that the adoption came too late. 'Twenty years earlier it might have been different, before your soul withered in you and mine withered because yours had. But it came too late. We had made separate graves for ourselves by then.' This loneliness, this hunger for a love which self-interest has destroyed over the years, was to prove another significant theme in Friel's mature work.

The title of *To This Hard House* comes from *King Lear* (III. ii. 63). Kent steers Lear into a hovel out of the storm while he returns 'to this hard house, – / More harder than the stones whereof 'tis raised.' Friel's Lear figure is Daniel Stone, a sixty-two-year-old schoolteacher with three children. Although one powerful theme is undoubtedly 'filial ingratitude', the variations on Shakespeare's text are considerable. Indeed, the intertextuality prepares us for the sort of playing off and around established texts which is a distinctive feature of Friel's later work, for example the use made of Pirandello's *Six Characters in Search of an Author* in *The Loves of Cass McGuire* and *Faith Healer* or the use made of Chekhov's *Three Sisters* in *Aristocrats*. In *To This Hard House* the aging father, Stone, is convinced that his only loving child is Rita, who lives in England, while his two other children, Walter and Fiona, are cruel and treacherous. Walter is, indeed, all Stone thinks he is; he assumes the principalship of a school which necessitates the closing of Stone's own school, and he never pretends that this isn't happening. But Fiona, the youngest, is actually the Cordelia figure, and not Rita, and this is something Stone never recognizes, even when – like Gloucester in Shakespeare's play – he goes blind. 'I have only one child left. But she was always the best of them . . . the kindest . . . the warmest . . . I know what I'll do, Lily; I'll write to Rita and she will come home when she knows we need her.' But Rita uses the money Stone sends to pay her passage to Canada. The play ends ironically, then, with the pathetic Stone finding no comfort in Fiona's return from London. It ends, indeed, with the lights going down on a recitation (just as *Translations* was to end in 1980). Stone's wife Lily reads to him to help him sleep, and her text is from *King Lear,* the passage where Lear rejoices in the prospect of imprisonment with Cordelia, 'Come, let's away to prison; / We too alone will sing like birds i' the cage', and so on for eleven lines (V. iii. 8–19). Stone never recognizes that Fiona is his real Cordelia. She too has been disappointed in love. For the man she ran away to marry never showed up but returned to their small town in Northern Ireland to set up a thriving minibus operation based on the new school. This is the kind of irony which marks off Friel's plays as distinctive.

In August 1960 Friel's first stage play, the unpublished *The Doubtful Paradise*, was staged by the Group Theatre in Belfast. Only the radio version of this text, broadcast in February 1962, seems to have survived. But this is sufficient to give a clear indication of the merits of the play. The radio version included a minuscule but significant change in the title from the definite to the indefinite article. Such is Friel's precision. For this is a play about a self-deceiver, Willie Logue, who lives in a 'fool's paradise'. He is the first of those articulate inventors who people Friel's plays and adaptations: a particularly good example is to be found in the autodidact Frank in *Molly Sweeney* (1994). Willie Logue too is an autodidact, who has 'the superb confidence of the half-educated'. He is a dangerous figure, a would-be poet in a small town, a post-office worker who is passed over for promotion while he engages in one educational scheme after another, the latest being the acquisition of the French language ('The Francophile' was another title given this play). It is hardly surprising that his sensible wife Maggie tires of Willie's incessant dreaming and the effects on his feckless children, as she bursts out: 'Stop it! I'm sick and tired of words and words and words. That's all I hear in this house – words and talk and talk and talk and words.' And she adds later, when the family crisis reveals Willie's incorrigibility: 'you could talk about anything under the sun and it never occurred to me that it was rubbish you were talking.' Of course, Maggie is right: like many of the women in these early plays she is a rock of sense. And yet what Friel had to do as playwright was to discount the Maggies of the world and to release into comic irresponsibility the Willie Logues of the world. Willie is a fantasist for whom the world as it is constituted in provincial Ireland would be intolerable were it not for the powers of invention. The paradise he inhabits may indeed be a 'doubtful' one and one injurious to those immediately dependent on him, but for him it is enabling; for him the renewable illusion is preferable to drab reality. And so he is a poet of sorts (a bad one, as Friel demonstrates) and as such he poses a problem for society. In his later, more successful plays Friel was always to find room for this unsettling type whose very presence signals the deficiencies in the culture to which he fails to accommodate himself.

The Enemy Within marked a major advance for Friel, not only because this play was staged at the Abbey Theatre (in August 1962) but also because here for the first time we find an assured style and sense of form. The three plays just discussed were all 'problem plays' in the old sense of that description: seriously exposing in a judgmental way the flaw at the core of some character within a hostile community. The struggle is between the individual and society, just as Ibsen and his successor Arthur Miller had placed it on the agenda for twentieth-century drama. The form of Friel's first plays, accordingly, is somewhat mechanical, as a momentum is created in the action which mounts to a figurative explosion and a cue for lengthy speeches of the self-revelatory kind. *The Enemy Within* is different. It is as much a study in patriotism as in sanctity; its interest lies in the conflict between the two. Columba, the sixth-century Irish saint, is depicted as torn between his vocation in Iona and his sense of loyalty to the tribal Irish in Ulster. As character study, this records a move towards the startling division of the psyche into Private Gar and Public Gar in *Philadelphia, Here I Come!* (1964). The dramatic form is of psychomachia or inner warfare. Here Friel seems indebted to T. S. Eliot's *Murder in the Cathedral* (1936), where 'acting is suffering, / And suffering action'. The drama in Eliot's play only comes to life when Thomas à Becket encounters four Tempters, the last of whom is the most dangerous because he represents Becket's secret desire for martyrdom. He must struggle against this improperly motivated desire until he sees '[his] way clear' and then Becket can await ('suffer') his destiny. Friel's Columba likewise has his tempters, and the greatest is within. And yet the plays are quite different. Columba is community-minded; his struggle is to give up politics, so to speak, for the family. He needs to learn how to stay at home and build a strong spiritual base: except that, paradoxically, 'home' here means 'exile'. He must learn, then, to make of exile a home. This, no doubt, is what the missionary life is basically about. But mostly in Friel's work exile is symptomatic of unbearable dislocation; it is in itself a spiritual state. To venture into this other territory is to venture into instability rather than into fulfilment. Thus *The Enemy Within* coins a metaphor which Friel was to recast repeatedly through many of his plays, down to *Dancing at Lughnasa* (1990), where Father Jack is a kind of grotesque version of Columba, and *Molly Sweeney,* where Molly describes her state of mind as a form of 'exile'. In contrast to many of these later exiled figures, Columba is a winner, and this is perhaps what makes him a saint. His are the last lines in the play: 'we are awake now and ready to begin again – to begin again – to begin again!' This is a rare, because positive, note for a play by Brian Friel to end on.

As is widely appreciated, Friel's major breakthrough as play-wright came with the production by Hilton Edwards in Dublin of *Philadelphia, Here I Come!* But before the writing of that play became possible there was one other piece of apprentice work which deserves comment here in a general attempt to outline the formation of an original playwright. *The Blind Mice* was staged at the Eblana Theatre in Dublin in February 1963. Its production did Friel little good and the text has not been published. Indeed, what survives is once again only the radio script of the transmission by BBC Northern Ireland Home Service, in November 1963. Yet once again there are elements and themes in this early play which serve to clarify Friel's ideas, even though Friel himself has disowned the play.

The Blind Mice is another play about a missionary, a priest in exile. But this time he is a modern religious, and as missionary to China he was captured and imprisoned by the communists. The play opens with his release after five years' captivity, followed by his return to a jubilant public in Northern Ireland. More like the later Father Jack in *Lughnasa* than like Columba, Father Chris Carroll is something of a 'fake'; indeed he is called such in the play. Because he signed a repudiation of Catholicism without having being physically tortured, the public (and family) attitude towards him shifts from triumphalism to riotous attack. The priest has betrayed his vocation. For the most part, this theme reflects the hysteria and rather alarming religiosity of a simplistic community, short on sympathy and extremely long on Catholic action. But the more interesting feature of the play lies in the study of Chris Carroll's guilt, not over his renunciation but over his loss of faith while in captivity. His despair is well described, and the loneliness from which it derived: 'I was abandoned! He had forgotten me! Can't you understand that? (*Calmer*) They talk about the anguish of despair. But it brought me a terrible calm. He had abandoned me; I abandoned Him. We were quits.' Instead of prayer Chris filled the void with nursery rhymes, including 'Three Blind Mice'. And he cannot move out of that state even after Father Rooney hears his confession. Chris's wrestling with his guilt, as he talks over his state of mind with the sympathetic Father Rooney, is Joycean in its intensity. Not since Joyce's *Exiles* (1918) has there been in Irish drama such fine Jesuitical calibration of temptation and of the agony of spiritual betrayal. More often, the priest in Irish drama is either a Fascist or a Pharisee: see the plays of Paul Vincent Carroll for the one and the later plays of Seán O'Casey for the other. Friel himself has never again drawn a priest sympathetically for the stage. The priest was to be either indifferent like Canon O'Byrne in *Philadelphia* or helpless like Father Tom in *Living Quarters* (1977) or cheerfully apostate like Father Jack in *Lughnasa*. In play after play the Catholic church is held responsible for the spiritual malaise debilitating Irish society. But in *The Blind Mice* Friel's sympathy was with the man of God deprived of his God. Perhaps, as Ulf Dantanus has suggested, the play was for Friel a personal exorcism, for he had spent two years studying for the priesthood in St Patrick's College, Maynooth. 'Perhaps the play was an attempt by Friel to de-church himself, to face honestly his own attitudes to religion and the priesthood.' If so, then *The Blind Mice* marks a major turning-point in Friel's work and art.

With the production of *Philadelphia, Here I Come!* in 1964, which reached Broadway for an extended run in 1965–66, Brian Friel's subtlety as artist became fully apparent. He subsumed into drama the arts of the short story and the radio play. Hence the sense of intimacy and the frequent use of monologue in the mature work. He began to show finesse in the interweaving of strands of plot material, the handling of those old bugbears of the drama, time and place, and the lyrical evocation of mood and states of feeling. Themes began to appear embedded in language rather than forced through with bludgeoning anxiety. Theatricality, as Patrick Burke has ably shown in his study of Friel's plays, became a priority over conventional dramatic structure. And the whole viability of theatre as a metaphor for the ambiguities and uncertainties of experience, of life itself, came as if miraculously into Friel's discourse.

Here is where Friel's own prose pieces and the interviews he occasionally gave can help the student form a truer understanding of the plays and their achievement. Time and again he will mention Tyrone Guthrie, the director under whom he studied (the word is hardly too academic) in Minneapolis in 1963–64. Guthrie liberated in Friel just those energies that enabled him to counterbalance dramatic intensity with theatrical flair. Guthrie's great emphasis was on theatre as ritual. He hoped, essentially, to reno-vate the modern theatre by doing away with the proscenium frame and returning drama to its Elizabethan and Greek roots. These roots, he was convinced, lay in religious ritual. He was mainly a director of Shakespeare's plays, and influenced what J. L. Styan calls 'the Shakespeare Revolution' in the twentieth cen-tury. The Irish plays he chose to direct were large, rugged and dif-ficult plays, like O'Casey's *The Bishop's Bonfire* (1955) and Eugene McCabe's *Swift* (1969), where the authors had something very specific, very disturbing, to say about Irish life. Friel certainly learned from Guthrie how best to address this business of critique: for that, in the end, is what Friel's plays constantly provide, a strong social critique by way of some ritualistic action.

Repeatedly, too, Friel refers or alludes in these prose pieces to T. S. Eliot and in particular to the essays 'Hamlet and his Prob-lems' and 'Tradition and the Individual Talent'. The former gave him that valuable working tool, the 'objective correlative'.

> The only way of expressing emotion in the form of art is by finding an 'objective correlative'; in other words, a set of objects, a situation, a chain of events which shall be the for-mula of *that* particular emotion; such that when the external facts, which must terminate in sensory experience, are given, the emotion is immediately evoked. If you examine any of Shakespeare's more successful tragedies, you will find this exact equivalence . . .

This notion, the opposite of romantic identification of artist and situation, has served Friel well. It has kept him clear of self-indulgent dramatized autobiography. It has ensured that whatever else may be said about his plays, each one contains a tight, sym-bolic situation which is essentially a contained metaphor which the action of the play will release into representative status. The feeling and the form tend to be congruent.

In 'Tradition and the Individual Talent' Eliot went further and insisted on the ascetic self-suppression of the artist's personal views and feelings. 'The progress of the artist is a continual self-sacrifice, a continual extinction of personality.' One sometimes hears the view that Friel is too buttoned up as artist, that he never lets fly with sexual abandon or sheer passion. The answer lies in his aesthetics, in his scrupulous control of the material. When occasionally he has felt that a play has had too much in it of feeling, insufficiently mastered by the form, he will comment on it in terms that are Eliotic. A notorious case is *The Freedom of the City* (1973), his play set in 1970 but patently, for all that, referring to Bloody Sunday. In his interviews with Eavan Boland in 1973 and with Fintan O'Toole in 1982, Friel clearly refers to Eliot's essay when he condemns his own failure adequately to filter from *The Freedom of the City* his anger at the time. Having used an image of a catalyst as analogy for the creative mind, Eliot argued that 'the mind of the mature poet differs from that of the immature one . . . by being a more finely perfected medium in which special, or very varied, feelings are at liberty to enter into new combinations.' If oxygen and sulphur dioxide are mixed in the presence of a filament of platinum, 'they form sulphurous acid'. This process happens only if the platinum is present, and yet the platinum neither surrenders any trace of itself nor is affected. Thus:

> The mind of the poet is the shred of platinum. It may partly or exclusively operate upon the experience of the man himself; but, the more perfect the artist, the more completely separate in him will be the man who suffers and the mind which creates; the more perfectly will the mind digest and transmute the passions which are its material.

Not only does Friel observe this concept himself but he uses it to portray the artist figure in his work. Francis Hardy in *Faith Healer* is just such an Eliotic figure, who sees the people he cures as his 'characters' but refuses anything like direct involvement with them or with those around him. Incidentally, Friel's acceptance of Eliot's theory should reinforce for us the notion that Friel is essentially a poet of and in the theatre.

What this means may be explained by suggesting that Friel is a stylist who combines two traditions. One is the Wildean tradition of wit, whereby perfection of phrasing and elegance of utterance are the aristocratic norm. The other is the Syngean tradition of incantation, whereby rhetoric establishes a democratic norm. In Wilde style is a measure of breeding; in Synge it is a measure of imaginative vitality. In Wilde wit is confined to the drawing-room; in Synge language thrives only in the outdoors. Wilde makes language a means of social discrimination; Synge insists – in *Deirdre of the Sorrows*, for instance – that a servant may be as eloquent as a king. By fusing the two traditions Friel provides a language at once polished and unreliant on dialectical exoticism and at the same time subversive of classical decorum. When Lily articulates what the moment before death was like for her in *The Freedom of the City* she finds a language far beyond the limitations traditionally imposed on a woman of her class. Critics sometimes fault Friel for what they see as a breach of good dramaturgy here, as if Lily were simply allowed to speak out of character. It is hardly likely that Friel did not know what he was doing. He clearly wanted a language of liberation here, through which Lily, shocked into recognition of lifelong deprivation, could somehow answer the glib sociological commentary of Professor Dodds. There is a politics to this use of language. Friel empowers his characters to meet and compete with a world of discourse dominated by professional talkers, academics and figures in authority. An obvious example is seen in Hugh in *Translations*, who, hedge-school master though he is, is allowed to speak like George Steiner on language and culture in order to maintain the dignity of the Irish argument against the British. The paradox may be that the tone of this surprising language is aristocratic. We have to remind ourselves at this point how often Friel uses that epithet with approval: Francis Hardy in *Faith Healer* sees himself as an aristocrat, 'if the term doesn't offend you', and the play *Aristocrats* redefines the term so that its older, imperialistic connotations yield to a contemporary, liberating individualism. There is, no doubt, something programmatic in this use of language. The closest parallel may be found in Eugene O'Neill, forever in quest of a language adequate to the modern American experience. In a key speech in *Long Day's Journey into Night* (1956), O'Neill's spokesman Edmund declares that the best language he can find falls short of poetry and is a kind of 'stammering . . . the native eloquence of us fog people.' O'Neill was working strictly within the confines of what Edmund here calls 'faithful realism'. But Friel breaks through this fourth wall and endows his characters with a 'native eloquence' which transcends stammering just as Lily Doherty does, or Cass McGuire, or most of the characters in

Dancing at Lughnasa. By enabling his characters linguistically, Friel dismantles borders keeping peasants in their place.

Another theme raised by the prose pieces and interviews is late-twentieth-century uncertainty. Here the early play already decribed, *The Blind Mice*, is a useful adjunct. In an interesting passage, Father Chris Carroll, accused of betraying the truth, declares wearily: 'I scarcely know what the truth is now.' For a Beckett character to come out with such a confession in 1963 would not have been in the least startling; indeed, the only startling thing about it would be that it needed to be said at all. But we need always to remind ourselves that Friel's plays are firmly, sociologically rooted in Irish soil. He is always attempting to represent what he calls the 'flux' or spiritual turmoil in Irish life after 1960. Thus, for a priest to concede agnosticism in the highly conservative Catholic society imagined by Friel is a wholly different proposition from Beckettian ennui. It carries enormous implications for the direction in which traditional belief was to travel in Ireland after Vatican Two. In *The Blind Mice* Friel seems to show that the game was not worth the candle, if religious belief is indistinguishable from neurosis on the one hand and sectarianism on the other. And yet there is an anguish in that play, what Tennessee Williams would call an 'outcry'. But other Irish playwrights, notably Tom Murphy, John B. Keane and Michael Harding, were to make this crisis central to their work. It is a key issue in changing Ireland. After *The Blind Mice* Friel addressed it in wider terms, with universal implications. Thus, when Gar O'Donnell ends *Philadelphia* with the confused confession that he does not know why he is emigrating, we have Friel's more mature preoccupation with agnosticism. The guidelines are disappearing; the authority figures are no longer in communication; uncertainty induces solipsism. I have written elsewhere on the kinship Friel's treatment of this mental state of things has with Pirandello's drama. It may be fruitful to compare also Pirandello's use of the theatre as metaphor for the illusionary nature of experience with Friel's *Faith Healer* or *Living Quarters*. Pirandello's pessimism, made astringent by his humour, has its counterpart in Friel's work. But the central point remains: Friel's main concern is to take the spiritual pulse of the Irish people, and to find the dramatic form that will render the condition of universal interest.

Attention paid to his essays on modern drama will provide valuable insights into the problems involved here.

Finally, to refer again to the various notes from Friel's 'Sporadic Diary'. These illuminate the process of playwriting itself. Valuable though this material is for readings of *Aristocrats*, *Translations*, *Molly Sweeney* and *Give Me Your Answer, Do!*, they must, I believe, be taken alongside the Frielian credo of impersonality derived from T. S. Eliot and discussed above. Readers would do well not to take these notes as prescriptive. Rather, they may be seen to record in a graphic and moving way how a Friel play germinates and slowly defines itself. In their own way they illustrate the problem of communication that Friel's plays in general so often enact. They negotiate between 'privacies' in the manner of a play like *Translations*. The silences and awful gaps when nothing is happening are recorded as honestly as the energetic leaps into fruitful composition. It may be as important to attend to the evidence of the waiting process as to those indispensable titles of books and sources that Friel cites as part of his preliminary reading.

We are reminded of the vulnerability of the artist, of the despair that is never far away from the writer's desk, of the horror reflected by the blank page and by the 'necessary uncertainty' of that condition. This last phrase is from *Give Me Your Answer, Do!*, Friel's only play about a writer, although he had written earlier about the artist in general in *Faith Healer*. The latest diary extracts, more veiled than usual, suggest the writer's need to discover his subject-matter afresh every time and how to give it life. In *Timon of Athens* the Poet claims that poetry is 'as a gum which oozes / From whence 'tis nourished' (I.i.21-22), but in contemplating his bees Friel does not find the writer's task quite so automatic. The honey-making requires both art and nature, planning and failure. The angst attending creativity is inescapable. Milton speaks in the proem to *Paradise Lost* of the Holy Spirit sitting 'brooding on the vast abyss' to make it 'pregnant' with the world itself: this is the writer's own challenge, and 'brooding' is exactly what Friel writes about in these diary extracts. In *Give Me Your Answer, Do!*, however, the relationship between the writer and his pain is bound up with silence on the one hand and the temptation of Mammon on the other. What Friel concludes is characteristic: the stoical response is the artist's only choice. Or, as the novelist Tom Connolly puts it *in Give Me Your Answer, Do!*, 'Be faithful to the routine gestures and the bigger thing will come to you.' In a sense, this is the rationale behind all the diary extracts. But, as ever, the play is the thing (in itself), the artistic victory over the very conditions the plot presents as insuperable. In such links between experience and art, the raw and the cooked, we come to know and love the man who strives always to maintain that battle line between personal suffering and artistic achievement.

CHRISTOPHER MURRAY

Works Cited

Andrews, Elmer, *The Art of Brian Friel: Neither Reality Nor Dreams* (London: Macmillan, 1995)

Beckett, Samuel, *Proust and Three Dialogues* (London: Calder, 1965)

Burke, Patrick, 'The Plays of Brian Friel: Theatricality and Technique', Ph.D. diss., University College Dublin, 1990

Dantanus, Ulf, *Brian Friel: The Growth of an Irish Dramatist* (Göteborg: Acta Universitatis Gothoburgensis, 1985)

Dantanus, Ulf, *Brian Friel: Dramatist* (London: Faber and Faber, 1988)

Eliot, T. S., *Murder in the Cathedral* (London: Faber and Faber, 1935)

Eliot, T. S., *The Sacred Wood: Essays on Poetry and Criticism* (London: Methuen, 1960)

Friel, Brian, *A Sort of Freedom* (Typescript, BBC Northern Ireland Home Service, 1958)

Friel, Brian, *To This Hard House* (Typescript, BBC Northern Ireland Home Service, 1958)

Friel, Brian, *A Doubtful Paradise* (Typescript, BBC Northern Ireland Home Service, 1962)

Friel, Brian, *The Blind Mice* (Typescript, BBC Northern Ireland Home Service, 1963)

Friel, Brian, *The Enemy Within: A Play in Three Acts*, The Irish Play Series (Newark, DE: Proscenium Press, 1975)

Friel, Brian, *Selected Plays* (London and Boston: Faber and Faber, 1984)

Kerwin, William (ed.), *Brian Friel: A Collection of Essays* (New York: Garland, 1997)

Maxwell, D. E. S., *Brian Friel* (Lewisburg: Bucknell University Press, 1973)

Murray, Christopher, 'Pirandello and Brian Friel: Some Affinities', *Le due trilogie Pirandelliane*, ed. John C. Barnes and Stefano Milioto (Palermo: Palumbo, 1992), pp. 207–15

O'Brien, George, *Brian Friel* (Boston: Twayne, 1979; Dublin: Gill and Macmillan, 1980)

O'Brien, George, *Brian Friel: A Reference Guide 1962–1992* (New York: G. K. Hall, 1995)

O'Neill, Eugene, *Long Day's Journey into Night* (New Haven: Yale University Press, 1956)

Peacock, Alan J. (ed.), *The Achievement of Brian Friel* (Gerrards Cross; Colin Smythe, 1993)

Pine, Richard, *Brian Friel and Ireland's Drama* (London: Routledge, 1990)

In Interview with Peter Lennon (1964)

Before writing *Philadelphia, Here I Come!*, which was the undisputed hit of the Dublin Theatre Festival, Brian Friel had already acquired a modest international reputation with his *New Yorker* stories and two plays. His first play, *The Blind Mice*, has been on BBC television; his second, *The Enemy Within*, had brief life at the Abbey, Dublin. A collection of short stories, *A Saucer of Larks*, published that year [1962], won critical acclaim both in England and the United States.

Friel is a former schoolteacher from Omagh, an old garrison town in the predominantly Catholic county of Tyrone. Married with three children he gave up his teaching job in Derry to concentrate on writing when he landed a contract with *The New Yorker*. He is thirty-five.

Peter Lennon: Are you a practising Catholic?
Brian Friel: I am. I was in Maynooth even, for two years, when I was sixteen. An awful experience, it nearly drove me cracked. It is one thing I want to forget. I never talk about it – the priesthood. You know the kind of Catholicism we have in this country: it's unique. Then I got a job teaching with the Christian Brothers which was nearly as bad as Maynooth. I was with them for ten years. Then I gave it up altogether. Last year I got an Arts Council award of £1,000 to go to Tyrone Guthrie's theatre in Minneapolis. I was there for six months. I had no real function, but the Americans handed me that nice label 'an observer'.
PL: And today?
BF: I live in Derry now. I'm a nationalist too, you know. I feel very emotionally about this country. I wouldn't attempt to rationalize about my feelings, but I get myself involved in stupid controversies about the border . . . I don't know why.
PL: You had a play on stage before that, before 1963?

BF: I had two. The first of these, *The Blind Mice*, was very poor. No, I'm not being modest. It's a play I'm sorry about. You know the way it is: you think you have something but somehow it does not work. It was a good theme. An Irish missionary comes home to the North after signing a 'confession' in a Communist concentration camp. It describes how people react when they find out. It was too solemn, too intense; I wanted to hit at too many things. I know now that people who go all flowery aren't going to get anywhere.

Some people think that if they write a play and get it put on at the Gaiety they'll change the world. But while you may move a lot of people for the moment there will be only a very few who will think about it afterwards. Maybe lie awake in bed for half an hour thinking over what you said. That's all I want. You are never going to move people intellectually in the theatre. If there is one thing I learned from Tyrone Guthrie it's that people at the theatre are moved by their hearts and their stomachs. As Brendan Behan said to me once: 'make them laugh and then stick them'.

PL: And the other play, the second play?

BF: *The Enemy Within* was about Saint Columba. It was a realistic play with no 'thees' and 'thous' in it. Saint Columba was a thick, big, 'get' of a fellow. I think he was anyway, and he was responsible for a hell of a lot of wars and butchery. I wanted to discover how he acquired sanctity. Sanctity in the sense of a man having tremendous integrity and the courage to back it up. In that sense Joyce was probably a saint.

PL: And how did he acquire integrity?

BF: By turning his back on Ireland and on his family.

PL: Isn't that the theme of *Philadelphia*?

BF: Yes. Gareth was leaving home not only in a local sense but in a spiritual sense too. Even if his inarticulate father had responded to him at the crucial moment it would only have postponed the departure. He would have had to get away. I took that quotation from the Bible, the 'enemy within', as meaning literally Saint Columba's family. You have to get away from a corrupting influence. I think in Ireland we feed on each other a lot; we batten on each other. But the corruption I'm talking about, a man finds anywhere around him – in Dublin or in Winesburg, Ohio.

PL: *Philadelphia, Here I Come!* is a rather subtle and gentle play.

Did you have any problems with the interpretation?

BF: It's really an angry play. It was very raw at the beginning but I toned it down. Then Hilton Edwards, the producer, is an Englishman. He did a very fine job but there were some things he found it hard to grasp. For example, the man travelling around with the Irish couple from America.

He wanted to know what relationship this man had with the woman – or even with the husband. But there was no definite relationship. I think you find that a lot in Irish marriages: there is another man floating like a satellite around the couple. A person in whom the wife confides, probably. There is nothing sinister in this and certainly nothing sexual, but English people would find that very hard to grasp. And people want to know whether Gareth's old girlfriend who comes to say goodbye is still in love with him even though she is now married and a mother.

But in Ireland many people would never admit such a possibility. They pull down the blinds. The Irish mind has many windows and the blinds are often down. In England they might have made love and it would have been tragic – or worse, they might have made love and it would have made no difference. But not in Ireland.

PL: Do you think Ireland is a good place to work?

BF: Dublin isn't. In Dublin your friends are legion – apparently. And it is too self-consciously literary. There is too much cheap chat. But you notice the amount of work that comes out of Dublin is negligible. I can work better in Derry.

PL: But in a small town would people not interfere more?

BF: Ach, no. They are more concerned about how you dress or whether you shave in the morning.

In Interview with Graham Morison (1965)

Graham Morison: I gather that you have just returned from a visit to New York in connection with a production later this year of *Philadelphia, Here I Come!*. When did you write your earlier play, *The Enemy Within*?

Brian Friel: I'm very bad on dates – I would think about three years ago.

GM: Have you been writing many short stories since that play or have you been concentrating on the theatre?

BF: I don't concentrate on the theatre at all. I live on short stories. This is where my living comes from. As for play-writing, it began as a sort of self-indulgence and then eventually I got caught up more and more in it. But the short story is the basis of all the work I do.

GM: Doesn't a play tend to involve the writer too much?

BF: The short story is more self-contained. You write a short story and you're totally responsible for it. You can delude yourself that the people who read it think exactly as you think and are highly appreciative. It never occurs to you that it's being read by people in dentists' waiting rooms or waiting for a train.

GM: While writing, do you have an ideal reader in mind?

BF: I don't think you have anybody specifically in mind. You try to be as lucid as you possibly can and you try to be as attractive as you can. I wouldn't put it any more rigidly than that.

GM: But you must entertain?

BF: Yes. And you must keep the reader with you. You can't risk that he throws the damn thing aside after two and a half paragraphs and says, 'I couldn't read any more of that.' But you must also persuade him to your point of view, to the particular vision of these people that you're writing about.

GM: Do you see the writer's job as one of breaking down barriers?

BF: No.

GM: I don't mean political or religious ones. But of getting one section of the community to take a closer look at another.

BF: I would agree with that. But never in the role of a crusader. I hope to encourage sympathy for the people I'm writing about. Sympathy and intelligence and understanding for these people. But never crusading for them, nor suggesting for a minute that these people I write about are more important than anybody else.

GM: Do you think that would be presumptuous?

BF: I do.

GM: What do you think of those plays that put across a social message?

BF: I don't agree with it at all. I think people like [Arnold] Wesker did a tremendous lot of good, though, and [John] Osborne, too; not for a class, but for the drama itself. Osborne rescued theatre and changed the direction of theatre. This doesn't mean that I think he's a major playwright by any means. He was an instrument in the course of the drama. He turned the direction of it. And was and is a good dramatist. But not a major dramatist, because I think that he lost something of himself through the cause he was fighting for – getting theatre away from Shaftesbury Avenue, or trying to do this.

GM: The new playwrights were often criticized for being more destructive than constructive. They never offered anything to replace the ruins.

BF: Well, of course – and I'm not defending Osborne in saying this – I don't think this is the writer's job. All any writer does, whether he's a dramatist or a short-story writer, is to spotlight a situation. In other words, he presents a set of people and a situation with a certain clarity and understanding and sympathy and as a result of this one should look at them more closely; and if one is moved then one should react accordingly. This is the responsibility of a reader or an audience, but I don't think it's the writer's.

GM: How do you want people to react? Do you want them to be angry?

BF: Anger is a theatrical technique. The theatre is altogether so different from a short story anyhow. You get a group of people sitting in an audience and they aren't individual thinking people any longer once they're in an audience. They are a corporate group who act in the same way as a mob reacts – emotionally and spontaneously.[1] Now you can move these people by making them angry. You can make them sympathetic. You can make them laugh. You can make them cry. You can do all these things. And this emotional reaction doesn't live very long, doesn't last very long; I mean, they will not storm out of a theatre and pull down a Government. Or they will not storm out of a theatre and build homes for people that haven't got houses. But there is always the chance that a few people will retain a certain amount of the spontaneous reaction that they experienced within the theatre building and that they will think about this when they come outside. And perhaps they may do something. But this is not the end purpose. The end purpose is to move them, and you will move them, in a theatre, anyhow, not through their head but through their heart. Brendan Behan used to say that you keep the people laughing in a theatre for five minutes and then in the sixth minute, when they're helpless laughing, you plug your message, if you want to plug a message.[2]

GM: In a short story, is it the characters or the plot that most interests you?

BF: It's both. It's the characters in a particular situation. It's these particular people, caught in these particular circumstances at this particular time. This is the basis for your short story. Now, if you can capture this with sufficient vividness and sufficient understanding, you will have seen them at a characteristic point in their lives and as a result of that you'll be able to gauge to an extent what they were like before this situation happened and you'll be able to forecast, generally, how they'll behave in the future. Obviously, you haven't got the time for character development in a short story so that how they're going to behave is naturally surmised. But I think it should be apparent from their actions and thought at the time you have captured them what their future is going to be like.

GM: What about place? There is a terrific emphasis on place in your work. For example, in the first story of *The Saucer of Larks*, the place is very important. Does that place exist?

BF: Well, almost. I couldn't point it out to you in a map, but I could point out four places that go to make up this one place. The general region, of course, is accurate. But the particular place within this general region is made up of three or four places within a broader area in the west of Donegal.

GM: Do you think a writer could go through all the elements of his story and identify their counterparts in his own past life?

BF: Yes.

GM: Do you have a strong memory, yourself?

BF: Not for everyday matters. After you've gone, I won't be able to remember the questions you've asked me.

GM: Do you have a strong memory of place?

BF: Yes. A memory of atmosphere, perhaps. The atmosphere of a place or the atmosphere of a person. They say, you know, that nothing important ever happens to you after you're ten or so. That could be very true. I'm a very strong believer in this theory, though I have never analysed it in any psychological sense. But I believe that it's very true. And I've also a strong belief in racial memory. This is a theory that Sean O'Faolain holds very dearly, and I think it's very true.

GM: It is said that a producer will often uncover strata of meaning in a play of which the author was unaware. Has this happened to you?

BF: No, but this is a theory that is widely held and generally accepted.

GM: Do you accept it?

BF: It could be true. But a certain arrogance keeps me from accepting it. This is about all I can say. I would like to think that I was fully conscious of every nuance of meaning that goes into everything I write; and I think: 'How dare anyone suggest that there's something in this that I don't understand fully!' But it's very likely true. For example, if ten people go into a room and look at a painting it'll mean perhaps ten different things. Maybe it's nothing more significant than that.

GM: What was your first play?

BF: The first play I did was called *This Doubtful Paradise*, and it was done in the Group Theatre in Belfast about six years ago. This was the old Group Theatre – before it collapsed.[3] It was a dreadful play. I don't think the Group Company collapsed because of it, but it didn't do them any good! It was a very bad play and I like to forget about it. Then I did *The Blind Mice*, which was also a bad play and which I have now withdrawn. The next one was *The Enemy Within*, which was a solid play.

GM: Are you happier about it?

BF: No, I'm not. It's not good, but it was a commendable sort of a play. I wouldn't put it any stronger than that. There's nothing very wrong with it and there's certainly nothing very good about it. It's a solid play.

GM: Did you ever find your plays getting out of hand? Characters running away?

BF: No, I don't believe this theory at all. Somebody was talking to me recently about this and maintained that the characters in her novels become dictators and she has no control over them. But I don't believe this. What can happen, however – and it's happened in a play I'm working on at the moment [presumably, *The Loves of Cass McGuire* – ed.] – is that you lose it halfway through. This doesn't mean that the characters have got out of hand. I've lost a certain excitement about it. I think maybe that in this particular case I worked too hard on it before I began writing it.

GM: Is this preparatory work mental?

BF: No, it's writing out notes – analyses of the different characters: what they did before the play opened and all sorts of details about them to get a very detailed knowledge of them. But I think that I overdid it this time. The result was I lost a certain interest in them: perhaps I got to know too much about them. The play is now half done and I haven't looked at it for the past six weeks. I've the feeling I've lost it. And three or four months' work.

GM: Do you often have to throw material overboard?

BF: No. But it has happened once with a play I did that was a complete write-off. I had to scrap it altogether. It doesn't happen often in the case of the short story. I've written a lot of short stories that are bad. Very bad. Stories that appeared in the collection *The Saucer of Larks* should never have gone into it. Many of them are not good at all. I regret that now.

GM: Are you more cautious now about letting your work see the light of day?

BF: Yes. There was a time when I could write ten stories a year without any great effort. Now I write four or five a year at the most. And even that is a great effort.

GM: Couldn't this be because you're not getting the same impetus to write as you used to?

BF: I'm not very inventive anyhow, at the best of times. Perhaps now I'm more critical. A lot of the stories that appeared in *The Saucer of Larks* and which I thought when I had done them were marvellous and were for all time, are utter rubbish, I can now see. When I am writing now I can detect this so much more easily and so much more quickly.

GM: When did you start writing?

BF: I imagine when I was about twenty-one. I'm thirty-six now.

GM: You weren't writing at school?

BF: Only the obligatory essays at weekends!

GM: You left school and went into teaching?

BF: Yes, well, first I was at Maynooth for two and a half years, left that and went to St Joseph's [Teacher Training College in Belfast] for their one-year graduate course.

GM: Were you writing then?

BF: I did a bit of journalism.

GM: This wasn't fiction, was it?

BF: Yes, I must have been doing stories. It's very hard to remember, you know. I think I did some stories then too. That was when I was about twenty, I imagine. It's a long time ago.

GM: You taught in Derry for about ten years?

BF: Yes, I stopped in 1960.

GM: When did you get your first story published?

BF: The first story I ever published was in the *Bell Magazine* – it was an Irish 'little' magazine and had a very strong literary tradition. Its editors had included Sean O'Faolain and Peadar O'Donnell. It's dead now for ten years.

GM: Did you ever have any doubts about going into teaching?

BF: Well, no, though going to an ecclesiastical college was a very disturbing experience, I found I liked teaching very well. I suppose it was an obvious thing to do. I had a pass BA degree, which was useless for making a career. My father had been a teacher; two sisters were teachers. It was the obvious and easy thing to slip into. And I liked it very well. Loved it. I was very lucky.

GM: Then you were running two careers?

BF: I was writing more and more while I was teaching. And it got to the stage when I had to decide which I would do.

GM: What swung the balance?

BF: £250. This is what I had in capital and I decided I could live on that for, say, six months or so.

GM: This was a bit of a risk to take, surely?

BF: Well, people say it was a very courageous thing to do. I don't see anything courageous about it.

GM: You must have had a great confidence in yourself at the time.

BF: No, I don't think so. I don't agree with this at all.

GM: Did you consider when you gave up teaching that you might be coming back to it sometime?

BF: Oh, yes. I was quite prepared for this in fact. I was sure I couldn't make a living as a writer. In fact this doubt has only been removed within the past year and a half. And it still could happen. If I were ill for six months, I'd be in serious financial bother again.

GM: There's no real security at all for the creative artist.

BF: This is the anxiety. And it's a constant anxiety. Even when I've made some money on a story this worry is always there. The £250 comes back to me now. While I was teaching, any money I made in writing was always spent on silly things like buying a fridge or something like that. And then eventually I said, well this is stupid, living like this; we'll save up whatever money I make. And when I had this amount of money, I said, 'Right!' Of course, what happened then was I was able to do a lot more work. You were fresh when you began working in the morning. It was what the Americans call 'moonlighting' – having a second job. Of course, it isn't off the cards that I might still have to go back to teaching. But it doesn't disturb me. On the other hand, I'm lucky to the extent that most of my work sells in America, which means I get paid by American standards. Living here in Ireland costs about a third of what it does in America. I couldn't live in America on what I earn in American money.

GM: Apart from financial considerations, would you like to live in America?

BF: I'd be very lonely, I think, in the way a child is lonely. I get very nostalgic and very homesick.

GM: What is the longest time you have spent in America?

BF: I was out there for four months.

GM: Without the family?

BF: I was part of the time on my own and then Anne and the children came out. I was at the Guthrie Theatre in Minneapolis.

GM: Is Tyrone Guthrie there permanently?

BF: The theatre is called the Tyrone Guthrie Theatre and he is artistic director. They do four plays each season and this year he is doing one. He's doing one next year too.

GM: He's a man who seems to be everywhere at the one time.

BF: He is. He's a marvellous, marvellous man. He's the 'greatest'. A great man in every way. Not only a great man of the theatre but a great man without qualification.

GM: When you're at home here, working, do you have a working schedule?

BF: In theory I have a schedule, which I never once hit. Roughly, the schedule is that I work from, say, half-nine in the morning until lunch-time – that's about twelve o'clock. And then maybe from half-one until three o'clock. But I never, ever, hit this schedule. I usually get upstairs about ten o'clock and answer letters. This takes me about an hour or so. And I try to get some work done then. Or else somebody calls. Or something else turns up. I may get an average three hours done in the day.

GM: How does your inspiration come?

BF: Oh, I haven't got any. Don't believe in it at all.

GM: Does this mean that when you're going to write a short story you simply sit down and say, 'Right, I'll write a short story'?

BF: No. This isn't how I work. This is an individual thing, of course. It varies from writer to writer. There's no set pattern for me. What I do is, I get an idea for a story. It could begin anywhere or with anything. It begins with the smallest possible idea which I write down in a notebook which I carry with me. And then I read this maybe three times a week. And then maybe after two months or three months I'll read it again and then I may fill in a few other details on the other side of the page. And then I'll leave this again. And maybe after three or four months I will then set to and start working on it. People say to me, 'How long does it take you to write a short story?' Well, you see, I can't answer that question. I don't know how long it takes. Generally I will spend three weeks in the actual writing of the story. Doing that and absolutely nothing else. Working at it, day after day.

GM: Do you actually write? In longhand?

BF: Yes, with a pencil. And then type it out myself afterwards.

GM: When it's typed out, is that it finished? Or can you still change it about?

BF: No, I'm usually finished when it's typed out.

GM: I've heard it said that a writer will often be able to view his work more objectively when it's typed out. Do you consciously become objective to your own writing after you have finished the composition of it?

BF: No. Not for maybe a year afterwards.

GM: Until after it's finished?

BF: Oh, long after it's printed. After it's printed I can read it and think that that's certainly not good, or something like this. But this is a long, long time afterwards. I find that you're so close to it and you're with this story for so long – it probably extends over a period of six months, I imagine – that you're not objective and cannot see the thing at all.

GM: You might be thinking of two or three stories running?

BF: Oh, yes. There are always two or three going at the same time. I've as many as twenty in my notebook at the moment. And if I get two out of them, this will be the height of it.

GM: So you often get bogus ideas down the left-hand page?

BF: Oh, of course.

GM: And you look at them in a couple of days and they mean nothing to you?

BF: Well, I always know what it meant at the time, but whether I can make anything of it or whether it can be developed and extended is another problem. There are very few editors that you can respect. My editor at *The New Yorker* is a writer himself, Roger Angell, a stepson of E. B. White. He has a book of short stories called *The Stone Arbour* – most of *The New Yorker* editors are short-story writers. And when he gets a story of mine, he may very often say that they just don't like it. But if he says that they like it, he may then suggest certain things about it. And, in that case, I will change the story. He always maintains that I understate stories, that I am always underwriting. I agree thoroughly with this because I think there's nothing as annoying as an overstated story. And it's a fault I have of underwriting. The result is that he often likes me to expand – frequently a last paragraph, which is the conclusion, the summing-up, the whole point of the thing. And if he likes a story he will very often write back and say something like, 'Right! this is fine. I am confused with the motivation of your last paragraph. Could you expand it slightly? You have the old man walking up the slipway from the harbour, looking back over his shoulder. But it isn't obvious why he is looking back. Perhaps you could just give us a line in there.' Very often, I think, Angell's right.

I'm talking about the ordinary changes made in a story. The sort of thing that people will level at you as a sinister criticism is to say, 'Do you change your stories for *The New Yorker*?' In other words, 'Do you produce a *New Yorker*-type story?' Well, no, I don't produce a *New Yorker*-type story, but I do change things for *The New Yorker*. I can't answer the question with a flat yes or no. But I will do this sort of thing: if I've used a word or a phrase that isn't intelligible to American readers, I would change it. It is my function to be intelligible to these people.

The editor will never suggest a major revision of a story. He'll just say, 'I'm sorry. This story isn't successful.' There are no other editors – no other magazines – that I would do this sort of thing for.

GM: Isn't the short-story market a very limited one?

BF: It is on this side of the Atlantic. It's a different thing over there.

GM: After *The New Yorker* I think of *The Saturday Evening Post*.

BF: Yes, I've had stories in *The Saturday Evening Post*. Mediocre stories. Well, first of all, they are always stories which *The New Yorker* rejects. I'm under contract to them.

GM: This means they have first refusal?

BF: Yes.

GM: It isn't a contract to produce and present to them a certain number of stories a year?

BF: No, no. There's no obligation at all. What they do is they pay you a retainer if you sign the contract and then they have to see everything that you write and they pay you twice as much as they would do if you weren't under contract.

GM: Well, it's no trouble for you to let them see your work first. I suppose it's quite an honour too that they think so highly of your work.

BF: Oh, of course, it's marvellous. If it weren't for *The New Yorker* I couldn't live. Couldn't live at all. And they're so – I hate to use the word – they're so respectful. It sounds a pompous thing to say, but you know what I mean in the context. They have such respect for work and for their contributors.

I think I'm sort of a peasant at heart. I'm certainly not 'citified' and I never will be. There are certain atmospheres which I find totally alien to me and I'm much more at ease in a rural setting.

GM: You would never think of going to live in New York?

BF: Oh, lord, no. I love it though. It's a very exciting place. I like American people. The pace of life is exciting – for a time. There's a great sense of unreality about it which I find very interesting. Somebody once said that when you're walking along underneath these vast skyscrapers, you feel that they're great Hollywood sets and that if you walk round to the back of them you'll see they're being held up by props and that they're only a front. And it's this unreality about the place which I find very exciting. They're a very interested people, too. People who are associated with writing or theatre are much more engaged than we are and not so ashamed of talking about it as we are. They have great dedication to their work.

GM: You mean they talk night and day about it?

BF: No, this is what they don't do. This is what you find very often in Dublin where they talk and talk and talk about their work. And, dammit, not a lot of work is produced in Dublin. Whereas in America there's not so much talk but there's a lot of work done. American actors, for example, all go in for callisthenics. Now, if you gathered a company together in Dublin to put on a play and suggested to them that for three-quarters of an hour before the rehearsal they do physical education – well, there'd be a mass walk-out. Yet this is a very important thing, because they've got to be physically very agile and on top of their form, especially for strenuous roles. This is a form of embarrassment which we have here, but which the Americans wouldn't have.

The Theatre of Hope and Despair (1967)

We have many illusions about the arts. We believe that they are a sort of gratuitous bonus that God grants to a prosperous society that works hard and is well integrated. We believe that they ought to be there when we want them – like taxis; that when we wish to concentrate on really serious things, like business, they should keep in the background – like children; that if they are worth their salt they should be self-supporting; and, above all, that they should entertain us. We ask of them that they should be a flattering reflection of the life we lead or think we lead; and we talk glibly and unwittingly of holding the mirror up to nature because we don't really know what that means. But our most persistent and most pernicious illusion about the arts is that they follow a pattern, that they have boom times and recession times which follow one another according to some unspecified law.

A boom time, we fondly imagine, is a period when lots and lots of jolly artists and craftsmen produce piles and piles of classical and everlasting work which in turn is eagerly patronized and bought up by scores of jolly merchant princes. And a lean time would be a period when crazy, would-be artistic types churn out a lot of rubbish that is unintelligible, chaotic, and – dammit – almost treasonable, stuff that no decent citizen could safely support. And in proof that such a regular pattern does exist, we look back in history and point out periods that were rich in poetry or sculpture, or we roll out fine phrases like 'the golden age of opera', or we talk about areas of time, as in Hitler's Germany, when, as we say, as if we had suffered a personal bereavement, 'the arts did not flourish.'

All this, of course, is nonsense. There is no pattern. There is no graph that rises and falls predictably according to any known law. And I am being contentious at the very beginning in case some of you expect that I'm going to talk like a professional critic, compiling one neat little pile of plays and labelling it Ibsenian – that is, having to do with or pertaining to Henrik Ibsen, and then another little pile and labelling it Absurd, and then placing delicate but sure stepping-stones between the two piles. Well, I'm not. The arts grow and wither and expand and contract erratically and sporadically. Like beachcombers or Irish tinkers they live precariously, existing from idea to idea, from theory to theory, from experiment to experiment. They do owe something to the immediately previous generation; they owe something to the tradition in which they grow; and they bear some relationship to current economic and political trends. But they are what they are at any given time and in any given place because of the condition and climate of thought that prevail at that time and in that place. And if the condition and climate are not right, the arts lift their tents and drift off to a new place.

Flux is their only constant; the crossroads their only home; impermanence their only yardstick. Once they realize that they have been so long in one site that they have come to be looked on as a distinct movement, that city hall is thinking of extending the town boundaries so that they can be absorbed into a comfortable community, they take fright, attack the movement – the apparent permanence – that they themselves have created, reject the offer of hospitality, and move to a new location. This is the only pattern of their existence: the persistence of the search; the discovery of a new concept; the analysis, exploration, exposition of that concept; the preaching of that gospel to reluctant ears; and then, when the first converts are made, the inevitable disillusion and dissatisfaction because the theory is already out of date or was simply a false dawn. And then the moving on; the continuing of the search; the flux. Impermanence is the only constant.

Within the past twelve months Leonard Bernstein was invited to England to conduct the London Symphony Orchestra in a series of three concerts. He chose Stravinsky's *The Rite of Spring*, the Fifth Symphony of Sibelius, and the Fifth Symphony of Shostakovich, and he called the series *The Twilight of the Symphony* because he said the symphonic form reached its peak at the end of the last century, and that in these three men who bridged the two centuries we had the final flowering of the symphony. In other words, the symphonic vein is worked out. It has nothing more to yield. There cannot be another crop. And he asked: Where does music go from here? *Musique concrète*? Atonal music? Who knows. All we know is that there is no going back.

In the field of the visual arts – of painting and sculpture – the flux is even more patent. Brillo boxes have long since taken the place of baskets of fruit, and Rauschenberg's goat with the tyre around its middle has replaced Henry Moore's reclining figures with holes in the middle. And in the field of the visual arts the search has become so feverish and the cries of *Voilà*! so shrill that we are all, I think, more than slightly bewildered. But an even more disturbing thing is happening in the visual arts. Since the war, movements as such are disappearing; or rather they occur so frequently and are so ephemeral that they can't be called movements at all. In other words, our nomadic painters and sculptors are so restless that they haven't time even to put up tents, and they find life so utterly puzzling and so quicksilver and so meaningless that no idea or concept can draw a substantial group of them together even for a period of five years. The result is confusion: for the artists themselves, isolation and loneliness; and for the rest of us, total bewilderment.

And as if things were not bad enough, questions about the nature of art are being asked that would have seemed heretical to our grandfathers, even to our fathers. For example, Nigel Gosling of the London *Observer* wonders why a work of art which moves, say, four million people in one year and is then promptly and for ever forgotten should be considered inferior to a work of art which moves four million people over, say, five hundred years. What he is suggesting, in fact, is that the capacity to survive time is not necessarily an essential of good art. And that *type* of argument is supported by your own Alfred Barr of the New York Museum of Modern Art who claims: 'It is folly to say what art is. Works can become art by fiat – sometimes the fiat of one man. And it can be art for a while and then not art. It is obvious today that comics are art.' And if I may quote another American in this context, this time the painter, Art Reinhardt: 'There is no place in art for life . . . the one thing to say about art is its breathlessness, lifelessness, deathlessness, contentlessness, formlessness, spacelessness, and timelessness.' I'm not too sure that I know what Mr Reinhardt means but I think you'll agree he's very much on the move, too.

And at last I come to theatre where, in comparison, things are almost stagnating. After all, in recent years, the only innovations have been Stanislavsky, Brecht, Freud, the Abbey Theatre, Ibsen, Shaw, Strindberg, Genet, Theatre of Cruelty, Theatre of the Absurd, Happenings, Black Comedy, Theatre of Fact, Disjunctive Theatre, and, finally, the Theatre of Hope and Despair, which I have been asked to speak about and which are not on the scene, but which the Thomas More Association and Rosary College presumably are cooking up in private. And before we get down to the current healthy and invigorating flux in the theatre, or attempt to speculate on the future, I would like in passing to nod in the direction of certain abiding rules which govern all theatrical enterprise. These are not basic aesthetic principles, and they do not apply to the other art forms, but they do have a bearing on the course that theatre follows.

The first nod of acknowledgement is to the cost of mounting even a modest theatrical production. This is not our concern at the moment. I merely wish to point out that a canvas covered with oils and hung on a wall is a painting. But a manuscript of a play in a desk drawer is not theatre.

My second and more reluctant nod is to Broadway and the West End, only because they are the accepted centres of Western theatre. They are, in fact, nothing of the sort. By and large they are merely warehouses where theatrical merchandise is bought and sold for profit.

And a final nod to the axiom that theatre can be experienced only in community with other people. One can stand alone in an art gallery and gaze for three hours at an El Greco; or one can sit alone in one's living room and listen to Mahler. But one cannot sit by himself in the stalls and be moved by a dramatic performance – and for this reason: that the dramatist does not write for one man; he writes for an audience, a collection of people. His technique is the very opposite of the short-story writer's or the novelist's. They function privately, man to man, a *personal* conversation. Everything they write has the implicit preface, 'Come here till I whisper in your ear.' But the dramatist functions through the group; not a personal conversation but a public address. His technique is the technique of the preacher and the politician. Every time a curtain rises, a dramatist begins, 'Ladies and gentlemen . . .' Of course his concern is to communicate with every individual in that audience, but he can do that only through the collective mind. If he cannot get the attention of that collective mind, hold it, persuade it, mesmerize it, manipulate it, he has lost everything. And this imposes strange restrictions on him because the collective mind is a peculiar mind. It is more formal. It is not as receptive to new theories. It is more simple, more spontaneous. But it is not as educated nor as sophisticated. And above all it is – or pretends to be – more easily shocked.

Let me put it this way. If I had a startling revolutionary idea I wished to propagate and if I were a slick propagandist, I could go down among you and, by talking to you individually, I could probably find four or five who would buy my idea or at least take it home on approbation. But if I were to preach that explosive idea from here, you collectively would be all so eager to prove how orthodox you are that I'd be lucky to escape without violence. And what relevance has all this to our discussion? It has this relevance: it means that in the present commercial theatrical set-up, the dramatist has got to be wary if he wishes to see his play produced and have people listen to him. He cannot *appear* to exhibit the same outrageous daring that the painter shows. It means that he must work more deviously than his fellow artist. It means that he must work more cautiously. And therefore, because of his indirection and his necessary caution and his obligatory deviousness, he is never going to be as ultra-modern, he is never going to be as apparently revolutionary. But, if he is of his time, his flux will be as integral but better camouflaged, his groping as earnest, his searching as sincere.

Sean O'Faolain has said that a writer is like an ant in a field. He scrambles up to the very top of the nearest blade of grass and trumpets to the world the unique truth he has discovered; and he trumpets with such passion that he doesn't notice that at the top of every other blade of grass in the field is another ant, broadcasting *his* unique truth. I think what O'Faolain says is very true. And I think there are two interesting things to be noted about modern dramatic ants: the first is the variety of instruments they use and the second is the sameness of the noise they produce.

What modern dramatists are saying is this. They say, with Nietzsche, that God is dead and that all traditional values died with

Him. They say that man can create new values only by becoming
God – that the only alternative to nihilism lies in revolt. They say,
with Camus, that this revolt is born of the spectacle of irrational-
ity, confronted with an unjust and incomprehensible condition.
They say that the Church as a divine institution is an absurdity and
that as a human institution it is an imposter, practising what it
doesn't preach and preaching what it doesn't practise; therefore, as
it stands, it must go. They say that the conventions, morals and
values of social organism that we know are all suspect. They reject
all the absolutes with capital letters – Freedom, Justice, Liberty,
Equality. They say that man comes from nothing, is going to nothing, and that in the interim period he should celebrate openly or
secretly what Robert Brustein calls 'the values of the extreme –
excess, instinct, emancipation, ecstasy, drunkenness, rapture,
revolt'.[1] 'Man', says Lucky in *Waiting for Godot*, 'in brief in spite
of the strides of alimentation and defecation is seen to waste and
pine waste and pine.' And since man's span of life is all that he has,
with nothing prior to take guidance from and nothing ultimate to
inspire or support him, since God is dead and with Him the tragic
hero, the only concern of the modern dramatist is man in society,
in conflict with community, government, academy, church, family
– and essentially in conflict with himself.

Take any modern play and look at the characters: two hired
gunmen, paid by someone we don't know, waiting to kill someone we don't know, for what reason we don't know;[2] customers
in a brothel who make believe they are a judge, a bishop, and a
general;[3] the inmates of an insane asylum;[4] drug addicts waiting
for a fix;[5] suburban dwellers who would appear to lead normal,
average lives, but who, in fact, are paralysed with fear and guilt
and anxiety;[6] pimps and prostitutes;[7] a corrupt police that con-
nives at crime, a corrupt judiciary that gives perverse decisions, a
corrupt government that provokes war, a corrupt pope with the
blood of millions of Jews on his hands;[8] two lesbians, one a BBC
producer, one an actress, fighting for the love of a bisexual
tramp;[9] two homosexual barbers groping frantically for a lasting
relationship between them.[10] These are the new dramatic heroes.

The world, according to the dramatists, is divided into two categories. There are the rulers – the establishment – who pretend to
believe in a traditional social structure that is Christian in origin,

that is now seen to be false, but which they still pretend to believe in, in order to give them the authority they require. And there are simply the rest – individuals, isolated, separated, sick and disillusioned with their inheritance, existing in the void created by their rejection, waiting without hope for a new social structure that will give a meaning to their lives. For a time it looked as if Communism – or even what we vaguely call the Left – might be the new messiah. But that, too, has failed. Everything has failed – politics, art, science, religion, philosophy. Man wastes and pines, wastes and pines.

It may be of passing consolation to this audience that the advocates of this metaphysical revolt and the plays I have so brutally summarized are almost all European: Brecht, Weiss, Pinter, Dürrenmatt, Orton, Marcus, Osborne. But before this consolation turns to smugness, I think it's also worth pointing out that there aren't sufficient American dramatic ants to constitute a species of its own.

And at this arbitrary point I would like to divert to make a few marginal comments that have a bearing on what I said earlier. One is that, of necessity, I have over-simplified. There are important individual dramatists – men like Wesker and Arden and your own Arthur Miller – whose view of life is by comparison not nearly so bleak. Albee, for example, is a very high-church Romantic. And the explanation of this may well be that an assured and wealthy country like America, conscious of its power and its dedication to probity, fashions its dramatists more thoroughly, and consequently will speak through them in a more optimistic, less dissenting voice; and that a poor, jaded, and weary Europe will find its expression more easily in dissonance and rebellion and disillusion.

The second comment I would like to make here is that European dramatists are becoming less indirect, less devious, less cautious; and because of this they are losing their general, family audiences and are attracting a much smaller audience of sympathetic participators. In many ways this is fine: communication between author and audience can be established instantly, and the mutual back-slapping is loud and clear. But if the dramatist is a propagandist – and he must be since he climbs up to the top of the blade of grass in the first place – he is preaching to the converted; and if he is really fired by a messianic zeal, the people he should be haranguing are the poor misguided fools who with their wives and children and uncles and aunts are laughing their silly heads off at *Cactus Flower*.[11]

And my last marginal comment is this: that although these modern dramatists would appear to be writing in a sort of unison, they could not be said to constitute a movement. Because, contradictory though it may seem, a movement implies a period of stability and uniformity: and our modern dramatists claim neither. Their only unity is dissension. Their only uniformity is their commitment to revolt and rejection. And that is why in this country they live uncomfortable lives in places like off-Broadway; and that is why in Europe theatre buildings are being made smaller and smaller. But in Europe there is this significant difference: that most of these uncommercial theatres are supported by public money.

And now to the future; as Bernstein asked of music: 'Where do we go from here?' The simple answer is that we just don't know. As I said at the beginning, flux is the only constant. But there are a few things we can be assured of. We can be certain, for example, that there is no going back; and by that I mean that the days of the solid, well-made play are gone, the play with a beginning, a middle, and an end, where in Act I a dozen carefully balanced characters are thrown into an arena and are presented with a problem, where in Act II they attack the problem and one another according to the Queensberry Rules of Drama, and in Act III the problem is cosily resolved and all concerned are a lot wiser, a little nobler, and preferably a bit sadder. And these plays are finished because we know that life is about as remote from a presentation-problem-resolution cycle as it can be.

And we can be assured, too, I think, that there will be a further exploration of shocking drama before it is recognized that it, too, is a false dawn. In other words, I think that for some time to come we will have a few persistent dramatists who will not rest until, for example, the sex act is performed on stage. And we will always have those dramatists of the moment who preach heterodoxy for no better reason than that heterodoxy will always have a following. But these people are of no abiding importance.

When I look into the future, then, there is only one firm prediction I can make, and it is this: that the gap between what I will call – for want of a better term – commercial theatre and serious theatre is going to become wider and wider. Broadway's dedication to smash hits and long runs will become more fervent, and this will have two results. One is that the audiences who go to the theatre will bring with them an ever-shrinking capacity for receptiveness and will eventually demand nothing more than a rudimentary and thoughtless entertainment, and shrewd business managements will simply satisfy that need. If you can evoke rapturous applause for stating that $2 + 2 = 4$, why venture into the labyrinths of pure mathematics? The second result is that 'serious' theatre will soon find that it can't get a foothold on Broadway at all; it won't get management support because it won't get audience support. And this, I think, is disastrous, because it is an extension of the fallacy that important things must be solemn, and because something is light-hearted it just can't be serious. I don't have to refute this to you. But I would like to remind you that theatre is by definition a *popular* art form. Euripides wrote for an audience of ten thousand; and in the jargon of *Variety*, if that isn't boffo, what in the name of God is? I believe that Neil Simon and Sam Beckett both have their place in the scale of things. And I am equally opposed to an exclusive diet of one or the other. I think that by confining one to Broadway and the other to precious art theatres in back streets, we do a considerable disservice to both gentlemen and a greater disservice to the public.

So again: what of the future? Have we had our Theatre of Despair, and against all the odds, is a pattern of balance going to emerge and are we due for a Theatre of Hope? In a very qualified sense I think a Theatre of Hope always exists and will grow stronger. By this I do not mean that dramatists are suddenly going to abandon their battle against the crippled civilization they find themselves in, and just as suddenly preach instant salvation for all who believe devoutly in the Great Society of America or in the European Economic Community. Nor do I mean for one minute that there is any sign of the modern dramatist losing his terrible, taunting questionings. When he says that governments are bungling, he's right. When he says the Church is fumbling, he's right. And when he depicts man as lost, groping, confused, anxious, disillusioned, he is expressing the secret and half-formed thoughts in all our hearts. All very fine, you'll say. But what is their positive message? They have whipped away all the scaffolding, all the crutches we depend on. And if they tell us that all our hopes are illusions, what hopes can they give us in return? Revolt, you say. But in support of what? You revile our concepts, you say. But what do you give us in their place?

The answer to these questions is that dramatists have no solutions. Furthermore, it is not their function to give answers. They are not marriage counsellors, nor father confessors, nor politicians, nor economists. What function have they, then? They have this function: they are vitally, persistently, and determinedly concerned with one man's insignificant place in the here-and-now world. They have the function to portray that one man's frustrations and hopes and anguishes and joys and miseries and pleasures with all the precision and accuracy and truth that they know; and by so doing help to make a community of individuals. They have this function – their supreme function, I think, and one they share with all groping, trumpeting artists everywhere and at all times, and it is this: that they recognize with great clarity the conflict between the world of the flesh and the world of the spirit, or if you dislike the terms, the world of the physical and the world of the cerebral. And when they depict in mean, gruesome detail only one portion of our existence, perhaps in this generation the dominant portion, they are crying out for recognition of the existence of something less ignoble, something more worthy. They are asking us to recognize that even in confusion and disillusion, strength and courage can exist, and that out of them can come a redemption of the human spirit.

'Mankind takes up only such problems as it can solve; since, looking at the matter more closely, we will always find that the problem itself arises only when the material conditions necessary for its solution already exist or are at least in the process of formation.' That quotation is from Karl Marx. And although he was talking of social revolution, it applies equally well to art. It could well be that many of the problems the Christian of today faces arise at this point in history because the solutions are at hand or are in the process of formation. Camus said: 'At the end of this darkness there will be a light which we have already conceived and for which we must fight in order to bring it into existence. In the middle of the ruins on the other side of nihilism we are preparing a renaissance. But few know it.'[12]

I am convinced that the dramatists are among the few.

In Interview with Desmond Rushe (1970)

Desmond Rushe: In most of your plays, *Philadelphia, Here I Come!* and *Lovers,* for instance, which have been performed in many countries, there is a lot of comedy and a great deal of human sorrow and misery. Is this how you see life in general?

Brian Friel: By nature I'm a bleak sort of person, and whatever comedy there is is the absurd sort. The only type of comic situation I see in life is a distortion of normality – which is a sort of definition of comedy.

DR: Have you always been like this – bleak?

BF: I don't think I'm getting bleaker as the years go on, but my view of life isn't very generous, isn't very tolerant.

DR: What have you seen in life to make you bleak and ungenerous?

BF: Now we're sort of dipping our toes into an area of philosophy in which I'm not expert at all. We all have such a brief period here in life, and the great portion of this time is spent either in working or crying. This general gloom is relieved only very seldom by periods of some kind of levity. I think this has got to be portrayed on the stage.

DR: Are you a pessimist, then?

BF: I don't know. Maybe I am.

DR: But do you not see something marvellous for the human being at the end of everything?

BF: You're talking in religious terms now?

DR: I'm talking in general terms. Can you really separate them?

BF: From the religious point of view, I'm a very confused man. The only thing that is of absolute importance is life – being alive and holding on to this condition of existence – but this in itself isn't really a cause for joy.

DR: Doesn't religion teach differently? That everything really worth anything is beyond life?

BF: This is heretical religion. And especially the Irish Church,

which teaches that the only thing worth living for is the afterlife –
this is total heresy. If there is an afterlife, the only way one can
merit it is by being totally involved in the here-and-now.

DR: Is there an afterlife?

BF: I have no answer to this. At the moment I don't know. As
soon as I make a ponderous statement, I'm usually embarrassed
by it the following week.

DR: What is your attitude to God – believer, agnostic or atheist?

BF: Oh, I'm not an atheist. I'm probably closer to agnosticism.
This is a very searching and groping sort of area where one can't
have any sort of scientific truth. You can't prove to me that there
is an afterlife, and I can't disprove that there isn't. So it really is an
area of speculation.

DR: Is it an area of importance to you?

BF: I don't think it's all that important. I am absolutely certain
that if I die next week and am going to go to heaven, I don't think
it's going to affect how I live here and now. I am not going to be
any more charitable or uncharitable than I am now. One tries to
live one's life as best one can. Let's forget about the afterlife for
the moment, and live this one.

DR: You were born and reared in the Irish Catholic tradition?

BF: I suppose I'm a sort of practising lapsed Catholic. It's one of
these attitudes I'm not prepared to defend, because I'm a volatile
sort of person, and next week I could be crawling up Croagh
Patrick on my knees. And I don't see any great contradiction in
this either.

DR: What is your background, Brian?

BF: I was born in Tyrone, outside Omagh, and lived there until I
was ten. Then we came to live in Derry, where my father was a
teacher.

DR: Your background was Catholic and nationalist?

BF: Very intensely nationalist, and in those days one's whole
nationalism and religion were constantly interwoven and inextrica-
ble. The result now is that while I'm not as intensely Irish Catholic
as I was, I'm still left with this very vigorous nationalism, as intense
as it always was. This hasn't much to do with the Border.

DR: It isn't just a matter of wanting a thirty-two-county Irish
Republic?

BF: The desirability of this isn't as obvious now as it was, because the turn the Republic has taken over the past nine or ten years has been distressing, very disquieting. We have become a tenth-rate image of America – a disaster for any country.

DR: What form does your nationalism take?

BF: There are certain values in this country which were very dominant fifty or sixty years ago and are well worth preserving. What we accepted as our cultural identity is certainly worth preserving.

DR: Do you want Ireland to get back to the old culture?

BF: One can never go back to the old culture, but it could extend to the present day. Our country should be as distinctive and individualistic as Belgium and Holland – I'm talking of small countries. Instead of that we're becoming more and more Madison Avenue-ish and slicker in a very shabby sort of way.

DR: What can you do about it? We are wide open to American influence, much more so than Holland or Belgium.

BF: I think, for instance, Ireland is politically sitting in the lap of America. We have never taken a stand on issues that were certainly moral – issues at the UN where [Frank] Aiken should have taken a stand and didn't. But to go back to what is going wrong. I think the emphasis is on having at least one car and preferably two. One has only to go into any of the posh Dublin hotels and one can see the new Ireland sprawled around in the lounges. This development is terrifying.

DR: Is this not an inevitable part of increasing prosperity?

BF: I don't see that it has any relationship with prosperity. One can have all the riches of the world and still have a very clean mind. It is sullied in Ireland at the moment.

DR: How would you go about cleaning it?

BF: One of the big problems is that there are two societies, and I feel very strongly about this. There is the Dublin society in the Dublin environs, and then there is the rest. This is not quite the same as purely urban–rural. You have an intensely urban society in Dublin, the cultural and political vanguard of everything that's thought and done; and you have the rest of the country living in complete isolation. The result is that instead of the rural and urban societies complementing one another and acting as a mutual balance, you have two distinct societies, one literally wilting away and the other forging ahead without this very necessary balance. A much closer link with rural roots is necessary.

DR: As a Catholic did you have problems growing up?

BF: Of course. As a young boy in Derry there were certain areas one didn't go into. I remember bringing shoes to the shoemaker's shop at the end of the street. This was a terrifying experience, because if the Protestant boys caught you in this kind of no-man's-land, they'd kill you. I have vivid memories when I was twelve or so of standing at my own front door and hoping the coast would be clear so I could dive over to the shop; and then, when I'd left the shoes in, waiting to see was the coast clear again. If you were caught, you were finished. It was absolutely terrifying. That sort of thing leaves scars for the rest of one's life.

DR: What do you think of politics?

BF: I try not to be cynical.

DR: Do you succeed?

BF: At the level of Irish politics I've succeeded, but looking at international politics, I think I fail.

DR: You took part in Civil Rights demonstrations in Derry. Did the situation there offend you?

BF: Until 5 October 1968, which was a red-letter day, I thought that society was absolutely dead. Then suddenly five young men, who had nothing to gain in temporal terms, organized a very shabby rally. The parallel is not accurate, but suddenly the whole thing was dignified, as in 1916. The police beat hell out of these fellows. And suddenly the conscience of Derry was aroused.

DR: You feel the Civil Rights Movement will succeed?

BF: What people are looking for is human rights at a very basic level, and I think they will possibly achieve these. But the danger is that they are losing something very important – their orientation towards an Irish Republic.

DR: You built yourself a house in Muff, County Donegal. Did you cross the Border deliberately?

BF: The Border has never been relevant to me. It has been an irritation, but I've never intellectually or emotionally accepted it. We had a cottage in west Donegal, so we've moved our permanent home into Donegal.

DR: If Muff was in the Six Counties, would you have built there?

BF: I don't think so. I would much prefer to be under the jurisdiction of the Dublin Government. Stormont is either absurd or iniquitous, probably both.

DR: You were, like your father, a schoolteacher?

BF: I taught for ten years in various schools and liked it very much.

DR: Before that you spent a term in Maynooth as a clerical student. Has that experience affected your life?

BF: I don't know. It's a very disturbing thing to happen to anyone. I don't know if one ever recovers totally from an immense experience of this nature. I was two years in Maynooth.

DR: Were they happy years?

BF: I wasn't very happy at the time, but I was sixteen or seventeen and these are carefree years. If one is to have a 'tragedy' in one's life, they are the best years to have it in.

DR: What do you think of religious matters at the moment? Have you any idea what might emerge?

BF: I've no idea, but I think this country is facing total chaos because of the complete stagnation of the hierarchy and clergy. They refuse to recognize that things are happening. Vital things are happening in the Church in Holland and America. I know quite a lot about the Catholic scene in America, where very interesting and exciting things are happening. The Irish clergy just dismiss it as just a Yankee fad, of no importance.

DR: What do you feel about the future of the Church in Ireland?

BF: Most likely the intellectuals will stay with it, but the mass of people will have gone. I find that the attitudes in Dublin are much more orthodox than I thought. The sermons I've heard in Dublin are a hundred years old. I would have regretted it some years ago, but now I don't care that much. It's a sort of spectator interest to me now. I'm not involved except at the level of education. In my own area I see children being taught in schools that are inadequate. I blame the Church for this, because they are insisting on special schools for their own kids. It is ridiculous.

DR: You gave up teaching to become a professional writer. What was your first published work?

BF: It should be a red-letter day in your life, but I don't remember.[1] I'd been doing a lot of reviewing and some journalism, and I had a few stories published. But the first major breakthrough I got was with *The New Yorker,* which is the best magazine in the world. When it took my first story this was a great encouragement.[2]

DR: What about your plays?

BF: My first play, *This Doubtful Paradise,* was produced in Belfast. Next there was *The Blind Mice, An Enemy Within, Philadelphia, Here I Come!, The Loves of Cass McGuire, Lovers* and *Crystal and Fox.*

DR: You have gone over completely from the short story to play-writing? They are two very different forms.

BF: I keep seeing close relationships between them, but I hope I haven't left short-story writing. It's a form I like very well. It's not as vulgar a form as the theatre, which is really a vulgar form of communication.

DR: This is because you are communicating *en masse?*

BF: Yes, and because the theatre and economics are so closely bound up – to such an extent that one is at the mercy of producers and managements. The commercial interests are immense. Not so bad in this country, which is good for a playwright. But it's awful in America. However, my experience in American theatre is only Broadway, and this isn't very fair to the country as a whole. There is very good regional theatre in America, but the Broadway theatre could not be lower. I'm not at all proud of having successes on Broadway, because I think it's of no importance whatever.

DR: It is financially.

BF: Financially it is of great importance. But I don't drive sports cars or have a yacht or a swimming pool or these things. I'm not even fond of good food.

DR: What play has given you most satisfaction?

BF: I couldn't answer that. All I can say is that I think the first part of *Lovers* is probably something I remember with a certain affection.

DR: Do you put yourself into your plays? When Eugene O'Neill finished *Long Day's Journey into Night* he said he had written it 'in tears and blood'.

BF: In writing you put all you've got into it, although it may be a complete failure. Inevitably, you must reveal yourself. There's a theory that actors fundamentally are very shy people and that they go into this profession because they want to hide behind the various characters they portray. I think that in much the same way a writer tries to disguise himself as best he can behind each play. In fact one is exposing oneself and at the same time hiding oneself.

DR: Do you write about things that you feel deeply about?

BF: These are the only things I could write about. What I would love to do in the next eighteen months or so is either a farce or a brilliant satire on Dublin life. Now I don't think I'm competent to do this, but I'd like to.[3] The very best way to treat the ills in Irish life is to satirize them.

DR: What playwrights do you admire?

BF: I admire Thornton Wilder immensely. He is one of the greatest dramatists of our time. For other reasons and other values, I admire people like Ibsen, O'Neill and a lot of English dramatists, Osborne, Arden and Wesker.

DR: What about Pinter?

BF: What I dislike about him is the complete dehydration of humanity in him. This is also something I don't like in Beckett. There is a complete abnegation of life in both [of] these men. They're really bleak! But life is all we have, you know.

DR: What about short-story writers?

BF: Frank O'Connor is superb. Outside Ireland, Updike, V. S. Pritchett and a Canadian-Italian writer called Vivanti.

DR: Do you particularly admire any twentieth-century Irish playwright?

BF: I admire Paul Vincent Carroll very much. And all the men, like George Shiels, who are, unhappily, going to be classified as less than great. But I'm not an O'Casey fan. This is a question of the urban versus the rural thing again. O'Casey is so intensely Dublin that I can admire him from a distance, but I'm never moved by him.

DR: You don't like Dublin, do you?

BF: Funny, I like coming to Dublin and I have a sort of romantic feeling – this is the capital and so forth. And very stupidly, I have a twinge of emotion when I pass the Post Office, because I admire the men of 1916.

DR: You write at a pretty high intellectual level, but your audience is, in the mass, unintellectual. Does the problem of communication with your audience worry you as a playwright?

BF: This is always a problem. If you deliberately write down, you court disaster. The most you can hope for is that you will hold their intelligent interest right up to the final curtain. At the end of any night's experience in the theatre, all that any writer can hope for is that maybe one dozen people have been moved ever so much or ever so slightly, and that the course of their lives may be enriched or altered by a very fine degree. I don't believe for one second that a dramatist is going to change the face of the earth.

DR: Why do you think people go to the theatre?

BF: I don't think they're going any longer simply for entertainment. They want to be engaged mentally, and if the dramatist does this, he is succeeding. The theatre is becoming more and more an intellectual exercise.

DR: Is the audience becoming more intellectual, then?

BF: Mass intellect is a very different thing to individual intellect. The group of people we call an audience is something like a mob,[4] and they're incapable of individual thought. But at the same time this mob has a different kind of attitude to the one they had twenty or thirty years ago. They are more receptive to intellectual concepts.

DR: You said that the theme of *Crystal and Fox* was that love wasn't enough. Could you clarify that?

BF: I feel in this age, and particularly since the Vatican Council and Pope John, that the whole emphasis in Christian doctrine is that we must love. It has been taken up by the hippy movement – love is all; make love, not war – and I find this whole emphasis to be a very watery sort of humanism, and a very shabby sort of liberalism. I don't think it's an adequate basis on which to live out one's life at all.

DR: What do you want with it?

BF: When we talk about life, anyway, all we mean is what are the relationships between people and between nations. Now it isn't sufficient that one orientate one's life towards a belief and love. One must also live one's life on the basis of duty and what we call charity, dedication and the sterner sort of virtues.

DR: But if you really have love, do not these spring from it?

BF: All I'm saying is that I don't believe in the uniqueness or absolute validity of love. In fact I don't believe that if you are in love life is going to be made so much happier or easier. One still has got to bring these other sterner qualities to existence on any level.

DR: What do you place first among the sterner qualities?

BF: Probably some sort of altruism. Generosity of spirit is the quality we need most now.

RR: What type of life do you lead at Muff?

BF: I try to do about three hours' work at my desk every day, messing around with new ideas or working on a specific play or answering letters. I've got to take the kids to school and back. Then we have friends in at night, or we go out.

DR: Do you watch television?

BF: No, we haven't got television. I think all television – using the term accurately – is a vulgar thing.

DR: What do you like to do at night?

BF: Read, or listen to music. Wagner is my favourite. I suppose this is symptomatic of something. I don't know what.

DR: What do you think of modern pop music?

BF: I don't think it's of any importance whatever. I think the Beatles, for instance, are totally insignificant.

DR: What of modern composers of serious music?

BF: I don't understand them. I haven't learned the grammar of these men yet, and it's something one should do. A lot of modern music is like a lot of modern poetry – it has become intensely personal, and communication is diminished by this. A lot of these men aren't communicating with us any more.

DR: You have four daughters. What legacy would you like to leave them?

BF: I would hope they will find themselves jobs in which they will be happy and realize themselves. I would like to see their capabilities utilized and expanded.

DR: Are you yourself happy? You look very content.

BF: I'm told I look a lot of things – content, serene, placid, self-contained. But I'm not at all. I'm very jittery, vain, anxiety-ridden, worried and very uneasy. Am I happy? I don't know what happiness is. One has periods of contentment. I think we're all in a period of spiritual and political eclipse at the moment. We are all acutely conscious of this unrest and unease.

DR: Do you think something decent may emerge in the end?

BF: Maybe. Or it may end up in total obliteration. This is an equally possible conclusion; it's quite a proximate possibility. On the other hand, it may end up in a period of sunshine. I wouldn't know. I'm not too optimistic.

DR: Are you easily hurt?

BF: Yes. For instance, the critics can hurt you, but they can't flatter you. The flattery of critics washes off. Lack of loyalty hurts me. Loyalty must be total.

DR: Would you live outside Ireland?

BF: No, I don't think so. I don't like America at all. It still has some virtues and it's a very generous country. I loved it when I went there first and I was very enamoured of it, but this left me very rapidly. Now I dislike it very much. I don't like England. It's a country I just don't feel at ease in, although I admire it a lot. The English have a lot of admirable things.

DR: Have you any ambitions?

BF: No overriding one. Just to write plays and another short story. That's on the professional level. On a personal level I want my children to grow up and be realized in whatever they do. I want to be in touch with them.

DR: You have a satisfactory relationship with them?

BF: I have at this stage. The eldest is only twelve and she still thinks I'm quite intelligent. So the generation gap has not entered into it.

DR: Is there any person who influences you very much, whom you look up to?

BF: I suppose my wife. She has great loyalty and courage and generosity of spirit.

In Discussion with Fergus Linehan,
Hugh Leonard and John B. Keane (1970)

. . . **Brian Friel**: This goes back to your question again: can Irish plays be intelligible outside Ireland? And this ties up with what Hugh Leonard has said – that form is the craftsman's problem, but the content and form make up the whole evening in the theatre and so the problem really is the content at the moment. The form is each individual writer's own damnation and his own problem, and when you get a happy marriage of content and form, then you have a great play, hopefully. But the content of Irish plays at the moment is a big question mark. Of the three of us sitting at the table, I think Hugh Leonard is the only one of us who is moving in the right direction. John Keane is stuck with the peasants of Kerry. Hugh Leonard is writing about the would-be sophisticates of Dublin and its surroundings, and I am somewhere half-way between the two.

John B. Keane: You say that I am stuck with the peasants of Kerry. When you say 'peasants of Kerry' you forget that we were the first civilization in Europe.

BF: I don't use the term in a derogatory sense at all . . . You are reacting badly to what I said. I mean, *Philadelphia, Here I Come!* was about the peasants of Donegal. It's the same kind of thing. But the point is that these people are of interest to other people only because of their quaintness, not because of their universality.

JBK: But surely if a man lacks quaintness, he is not an individual any more? He must be quaint in some fashion. If he is going to be tied down and live in a boxy house and if he lives like a thousand others, it is the quaintness that attracts and that makes him different from any other man . . .

Fergus Linehan: Can I ask you each one final, perhaps glib, question? How would you like to see your own work developing?

. . . **BF**: You can only talk in general. I would like to write a play that would capture the peculiar spiritual and indeed material flux that this country is in at the moment. This has got to be done, for me anyway, and I think it has got to be done at a local, parochial level, and hopefully this will have meaning for other people in other countries . . .

Self-Portrait (1972)

Even a fragment of autobiography such as this is of necessity and by definition an exercise in exhibitionism, in exorcism, and in expiation. Of the three the element of exhibitionism will be least, but it usually takes the form not simply of showing off but of putting a good skin on – that is, of taking our trivial achievements and our abysmal failures and staging them in subtle lighting and in attractive costumes and hoping to God the performance comes off. The other two elements – the elements of exorcism and expiation – are the important ones, and they are really two sides of the same coin: because we call up our ghosts not to lay them but in the hope of having the genuine dialogue with them we didn't have when we had the opportunity. Then there are, of course, what are called the 'facts'; and since some people value the tidiness they seem to afford, let's have the facts first and be done with them.

I was born in Omagh in County Tyrone in 1929. My father was principal of a three-teacher school outside the town. He taught me. In 1939, when I was ten, we moved to Derry where I have lived since, until three or four years ago. I was at St Columb's College for five years, St Patrick's College, Maynooth, for two and a half years, and St Joseph's Training College for one year. From 1950 until 1960 I taught in various schools around Derry. Since then I have been writing full-time.

I am married, have five children, live in the country, smoke too much, fish a bit, read a lot, worry a lot, get involved in sporadic causes and invariably regret the involvement, and hope that between now and my death I will have acquired a religion, a philosophy, a sense of life that will make the end less frightening than it appears to me at this moment. What other facts are there? – Ah, the interviewer's chestnut: When did you know you were going to be a writer? The answer is, I've no idea. What other writers influenced you most strongly? I've no idea. Which of your plays is your favourite? None of them. Which of your stories? Most of them embarrass me. Do you think the atmosphere in Ireland is hostile or friendly to the artist? I'm thinking of my lunch. Do you see any relationship between dwindling theatrical audiences all over the world and the fragmentation of what we might call the theatrical thrust into disparate movements like Theatre of Cruelty, Tactile Theatre, Nude Theatre, Theatre of Despair, etc. etc? Or would you say, Mr Friel, that the influence of Heidegger is only beginning to be felt in the drama and that Beckett and Pinter are John the Baptists of a great new movement? Well, in answer to that I'd say that – I'd say that I'm a middle-aged man and that I tire easily and that I'd like to go out for a walk now, so please go away and leave me alone.

The facts. What is a fact in the context of autobiography? A fact is something that happened to me or something I experienced. It can also be something I thought happened to me, something I thought I experienced. Or indeed an autobiographical fact can be pure fiction and no less true or reliable for that. Let me give an example.

When I was a boy we always spent a portion of our summer holidays in my mother's old home near the village of Glenties in County Donegal. I have memories of those holidays that are as pellucid, as intense, as if they happened last week. I remember in detail the shape of cups hanging in the scullery, the pattern of flags on the kitchen floor, every knot of wood on the wooden stairway, every door handle, every smell, the shape and texture of every tree around the place. My father and I used to go fishing on the lakes near the village. There were about eight of them we used to go to. And although I haven't seen them for twenty-five years I know them with a knowledge that is special and sacred and so private that it is almost apprehensive. But what I want to talk about now is a particular memory of a particular day. There's no doubt in my mind about this – it's here now before my eyes as I speak. The boy I see is about nine years old and my father would have been in his early forties. We are walking home from a lake with our fishing rods across our shoulders. It has been raining all day long; it is now late evening; and we are soaked to the skin. But for some reason – perhaps the fishing was good – I don't remember – my father is in great spirits and is singing a song and I am singing with him.

And there we are, the two of us, soaking wet, splashing along a muddy road that comes in at right angles to Glenties' main street, singing about how my boat can safely float through the teeth of wind and weather. That's the memory. That's what happened. A trivial episode without importance to anyone but me, just a moment of happiness caught in an album. But wait. There's something wrong here. I'm conscious of a dissonance, an unease. What is it? Yes, I know what it is: there is no lake along that muddy road. And since there is no lake my father and I never walked back from it in the rain with our rods across our shoulders. The fact is a fiction. Have I imagined the scene then? Or is it a composite of two or three different episodes? The point is – I don't think it matters. What matters is that for some reason – and we're back to our opening ideas of our expiation and exorcism – for some reason this vivid memory is there in the storehouse of the mind. For some reason the mind has shuffled the pieces of verifiable truth and composed a truth of its own. For to me it is a truth. And because I acknowledge its peculiar veracity, it becomes a layer in my subsoil; it becomes part of me; ultimately it becomes me.

Before I leave my childhood and youth I want to look back briefly at that bizarre process called my education. For about fifteen years I was taught by a succession of men who force-fed me with information, who cajoled me, beat me, threatened me, coaxed me to swallow their puny little pies of knowledge and attitudes.

And the whole thing, I know now, was an almost complete waste of time. I'm not resentful about this. I don't feel scarred or damaged by it. And I'm certainly not blaming these grim men who prodded me through examinations; they were victims as much as I. But surely this isn't education? Beginning at Tudor Reign – 1485; Diaz discovers the Cape – 1488; Columbus discovers America – 1492; Vasco da Gama discovers the Cape route to India – 1498. Or:

> Hence loathed Melancholy,
>   Of Cerberus and blackest midnight born
> In Stygian cave forlorn
>   'Mongst horrid shapes, and shrieks, and sights unholy,
> Find out some uncouth cell,
>   Where brooding Darkness spreads his jealous wings,
> And the night-raven sings;

There under ebon shades and low-brow'd rocks,
As ragged as thy locks,
In dark Cimmerian desert ever dwell.

That, incidentally, was John Milton. Or:

A rhomboid is an oblique-angled parallelogram with only the opposite sides equal.

Or:

> Arma virumque cano
> Troiae qui primus ab oris
> Italiam fato profugus Lavinaque venit litora.

['I sing of arms and the man who first among men in flight from Trojan lands was driven by fate to Italy and came to the Lavinian shores.' Opening lines of Virgil's *Aeneid*.]

And so on. And so on.

Yes, on second thoughts I am slightly resentful. And the little grudge I bear is directed against those men who taught me the literature of Rome and Greece and England and Ireland as if they were pieces of intricate machinery, created for no reason and designed for no purpose. They were called out of the air, these contrivances, and planked in front of us, and for years we tinkered with them, pulling them apart, putting them together again, translating, scanning, conjugating, never once suspecting that these texts were the testimony of sad, happy, assured, confused people like ourselves. And there we were, so engaged in irregular verbs and peculiar declensions that we never once smelt blood or felt gristle. Yes, I resent that slightly. Indeed, I was fairly long in the tooth before I made the modest discovery for myself that literature wasn't some kind of political dynasty where Elizabethans were ousted by Puritans who gave way to Restoration Dramatists who in turn were routed by the Augustans who were supplanted by the Romantics who were followed by Eminent Victorians, etc. etc.: some kind of literary monopoly invented by critics and academics for the torment of students.

I'm going to make a detour past those ten years when I taught school myself because I regret them, and there's nothing more boring or more boastful than a public confession of venial sins. I don't regret the teaching – in fact I liked teaching. At least I liked doing what I thought then was teaching; because what I was doing was putting boys in for maths exams and getting them through. In fact I fancied myself as a teacher because I worked hard at teaching the tricks and the poodle dogs became excellent performers. And I regret, too, that I used a strap. Indeed, I regret this most of all. It's a ghost I have called up many a time since but he still won't be atoned to. I suppose he's right.

And before I leave those ten years I might as well mention that this was when I first began to fumble with short stories and with plays. This was when I got married; this was the time when I first began to wonder what it was to be an Irish Catholic; in short this was when for the first time in my life I began to survey and analyse the mixed holding I had inherited: the personal, traditional and acquired knowledge that cocooned me, an Irish Catholic teacher with a nationalist background, living in a schizophrenic community, son of a teacher, grandson of peasants who could neither read nor write. The process was disquieting – is disquieting because it is still going on. But what I hope is emerging is, in the words of Sean O'Faolain, a faith, a feeling for life, a way of seeing life which is coherent, persistent, inclusive, and forceful enough to give organic form to the totality of my work.

But back to the facts. In the year 1960 I left teaching and, as they used to say, embarked on a career of letters. By then I had had some pale success with short stories and radio plays – and I'll come back to that chameleon word 'success' in a moment or two – and, by doing some journalism as well, I was making just about enough money to keep going.

And it was about that time that I had to make a decision. If you want to be a playwright, you must either arrange to be a child of theatrical parents and born preferably in the green-room in the interval between Act I and Act II of *Separate Tables*; or you will have to have been dragged to theatre matinées every Wednesday and Saturday by an eccentric maiden aunt; or have played the gravedigger in the school production of *Hamlet*; or at very least you will have to have been usher for the local amateur dramatic association. I was privileged in none of these ways. And now I found myself at thirty years of age embarked on a theatrical career and almost totally ignorant of the mechanics of play-writing and play-production apart from an intuitive knowledge. Like a painter who has never studied anatomy; like a composer with no training in harmony. So I packed my bags and with my wife and two children went to Minneapolis in Minnesota where a new theatre was being created by Tyrone Guthrie, and there I lived for six months.

That period is a story in itself. Immediately after it ended I thought it was the most important – or as they say now, traumatic – period I had ever experienced. And of course it was nothing of the kind. The really traumatic experiences are sly and dark and devious and generally slip into the consciousness through an unlocked window. But it was an important period in a practical way. I learned about the physical elements of plays, how they are designed, built, landscaped. I learned how actors thought, how they approached a text, their various ways of trying to realize it.

I learned a great deal about the iron discipline of theatre, and I discovered a dedication and a nobility and a selflessness that one associates with a theoretical priesthood. But much more important than all these, those months in America gave me a sense of liberation – remember, this was my first parole from inbred claustrophobic Ireland – and that sense of liberation conferred on me a valuable self-confidence and a necessary perspective so that the first play I wrote immediately after I came home, *Philadelphia, Here I Come!*, was a lot more assured than anything I had attempted before.

And now to return to that strange word 'success'. I have written nine plays, and of these two are classified as 'successful', more vulgarly as 'hits'. If one is to pursue this jargon the other seven plays are flops. For a writer these terms have no meaning – the word success has no meaning. I am not being at all obtuse or grandly aloof. People may like a play of mine or hate it – that is another question. It may be performed all over the world or just once in a basement theatre in Cork; it may be a well-constructed play or a badly constructed play; it may be simple or obscure – these are other considerations entirely. But for the writer there is no success just as there is no 'success' in the rain falling or the sun shining. In a strictly limited sense, yes, and only with reference to a hierarchy of values that have meaning only for the writer himself – then he can assess a play as successful. But what he means is something very different from public acclaim or press awards or best-seller lists.

What he means is that this particular work is in tune with the body of his previous work; that it is a forward step in the revelation of his relationship with his own world, and that at the time of writing the idea and form are coincidental and congruent and at one. Then he knows he has written a success and this knowledge is the only abiding satisfaction he has. Everything else is trivial.

What did I do in Minneapolis? The honest answer to that is very little. I lived in a languishing hotel called the Oak Grove and I spent my days and evenings in the theatre, literally skulking about in the gloom of the back seats. The Guthrie Theatre was a courageous concept – an attempt to establish a classical theatre in what is traditionally considered the philistine Mid-west and thousands of miles away from New York, which is the tawdry Mecca of American theatre. And because this was a pioneering effort determined to succeed, everybody was extraordinarily keen and dedicated and enthusiastic and busy. It was no place at all for a drone. For a few weeks I managed to make myself almost invisible. I slipped into the building with the workmen in the morning and slipped out with the actors at night. But eventually an obese and evil-looking stage doorman appropriately called Chuck stopped me and demanded to know my business. And just as I was stammering a garbled explanation one of the actors volunteered, 'He's okay, Chuck. He's an observer.' And that fortuitous christening instantly gave me not only an identity but a dignity: an observer, part of the great communal effort, pass, friend.

I moved from the gloom of the back row down to the orchestra. People began to nod to me. I got a pencil and paper and occasionally pretended to jot down profound observations. Some of the less secure actors even began to ask my advice about their performance, God help them. It was all very gratifying. But there were some disadvantages. Up to this I could crouch in the dark and scratch and grunt and make faces and mutter to myself. Now I had to sit in smart attention and gaze at the stage for hours on end. It was very, very tiring. When I got back to the Oak Grove at night it was hours before the muscles of my face would surrender the intelligent, alert look I had assumed all day. Observers may contribute little to the life of the theatre but they work harder than anyone else I know.

The years that followed immediately after that visit to Minneapolis were busy. I wrote five plays, watched over their launching in Dublin and travelled with them to London or New York for their first production outside the country. It would be churlish to say that it was all work and worry. It wasn't. There was a lot of fun, because theatre people are the best company in the world. I mean actors, of course, not impresarios who are mere hucksters in the merchandise of drama. But actors are a very special people. Their stock characteristics – their gaiety, their effusiveness, their temperaments, their easy charm, their volatile affections – all the things that most people dislike in them I find fascinating. I don't think their lives are 'unreal'. If there is such a thing as a 'real' life – and presumably a real life would be some kind of a lifestyle that would reflect the very essence and accidents of existence – then surely actors are much closer to that image than the nine-to-five businessman.

But there was worry, too. And the reason for the worry is that the playwright is never fully his own man. The painter completes his picture and the public look at his work on the gallery wall. The poet or novelist produces his book and through it talks directly to his reader. But the playwright requires interpreters. Without actors and without a performance his manuscript is a lifeless literary exercise, a kite without wind, a boat waiting for a tide. And the day he completes his script he has won a battle and taken on a war. First of all he has got to get a management to put on his play. He then has to get a director – and nowadays directors have pushed themselves into such power in the theatre that they expect writers not only to approach them with awe but to surrender the entire interpretation of a play into their artistic hands. Right. He gets a management, he gets a director, he gets his actors. Rehearsals begin. From here on the pain or the pleasure the writer experiences depends on his attitude to his director and to his actors. And my attitude is this. I look on my manuscript as an orchestral score, composed with infinite care and annotated where necessary with precise directions. This is in no way a judgment in quality but a statement of character.

I look to the director and the actors to interpret that score exactly as it is written. It is not their function to amend, it is not their function to rewrite, or to cut, or to extend. It is their function, their only function – and an enormously difficult one – to interpret what is given them. And I use the analogy of the orchestral score with deliberation because I have never known a conductor who would even dream of tampering with the shape of a symphony nor an instrumentalist who would think of rewriting a score before performing it; but I have yet to meet the director or the actor who wouldn't casually paraphrase lines of dialogue or indeed transpose whole scenes. Hence the war; or at least the twitching truce. Of course there are playwrights who will disagree with me, who are happy to rewrite on request during rehearsal, even after the play has opened; and their thesis is that theatre is a communal enterprise to which the writer, actor, and director contribute on a sort of ad hoc principle. One of their most dubious maxims is – if it works it's right. Well, of course, I think they're completely wrong. These people really belong in showbiz. But there are so many of them and they have such strong support from directors and actors that those of us who believe in the responsibility of the script are considered cranks and difficult to work with. So be it.

But to get back to the main thoroughfare. When I spoke earlier of a faith, a feeling for life, a way of seeing life, I was not of course talking of a schematized set of religious beliefs. I meant the patient assembly of a superstructure which imposes a discipline and within which work can be performed in the light of an insight, a group of ideas, a carefully cultivated attitude; or as Seamus Heaney puts it with less contortion: there are only certain stretches of ground over which the writer's divining rod will come to life.[1] And when I referred to Ireland as being inbred and claustrophobic, and talked of the tortuous task of surveying the mixed holding I had inherited, I had in mind how difficult it is for an Irish writer to find his faith: he is born into a certainty that is cast-iron and absolute. The generation of Irish writers immediately before mine never allowed this burden to weigh them down. They learned to speak Irish, took their genetic purity for granted, and soldiered on. For us today the situation is more complex. We are more concerned with defining our Irishness than with pursuing it. We want to know what the word 'native' means, what the word 'foreign' means. We want to know if the words have any meaning at all. And persistent considerations like these erode old certainties and help clear the building site.

People often urge me to write a play 'about the trouble[s] in the North'. You have the dramatic situation, they tell me; you have the conflict; you know the scene. As if this is what writing is about – take the do-it-yourself kit up to your study and assemble the pieces according to the enclosed leaflet.

But of course they are not really offering me the stuff of a play any more than the people who say to me, 'I'll tell you something that happened to me. If I had your talent I could make a damned good story out of it. What happened was this.' And they know they're offering me nothing, these people. All they're doing is to strut in front of me. They're saying: 'My life is full of excitement, not like yours; and if I only had the knack, if I only had the education, if I only had the time, I'm the buck would churn out the books.' There was a time when I thought these were well-meaning people. Perhaps they are. But now I think they're sad.

Exhibitionism. Exorcism. Expiation. In spite of my opening comment it seems to have been all ostentation, all parade, the swagger of the first person singular. But when you ask me have I anything to declare and I say, only this and this, I assume that you will look beyond the innocent outspread hands.

In Interview with Des Hickey and Gus Smith (1972)

. . . I began writing when I was about nineteen. I know that after *Philadelphia* it was said that I was a born writer, but I don't know what a born writer is. The craft of writing is something you learn painfully and slowly. There was no background of writing in my family and I don't know how much of my talent is indigenous. I don't think there were many other writers in Derry. Some people feel that if you are a writer or painter you must live in a colony, but I find writing a very private and personal existence and I was aware of no sense of loss at being the only writer in Derry. I was a full-time writer from 1960, writing mostly short stories in those days. I had been a teacher until then.

I began *Philadelphia* in 1962 or '63. It was a play about an area of Irish life that I had been closely associated with in County Donegal. Our neighbours and our friends there have all been affected by emigration, but I don't think the play specifically concerns the questions of emigration. *Philadelphia* was an analysis of a kind of love: the love between a father and a son and between a son and his birthplace. This is a theme I have tried to explore in three or four plays. *Cass McGuire*, *Lovers* and *Crystal and Fox* were all attempts at analysing different kinds of love. A writer does not look at his work on a vertical scale. He doesn't say that one play was better than another. In four plays I attempted to analyse a concept of love. In *Crystal and Fox* I reached a conclusion from my point of view; in other words, I had mined this vein to the end, and perhaps the vein was not rich enough. At any rate I reached a kind of completion and left this area to write a play in a completely new direction, *The Mundy Scheme*.

Other European countries have been warm and generous towards my plays, but not England. I think the English are unsympathetic to anything Irish. I don't mean this to be a chauvinistic comment; I believe the English refuse to take the Irish seriously on any issue. On the other hand, my respect for and interest in Broadway is nil. To me Broadway is an enormous warehouse in which dramatic merchandise is bought and sold at the highest possible profit. Occasionally good things happen there, but by and large it has nothing to do with the art of theatre.

People ask why I have not written a play about the civil rights movement. One answer is that I have no objectivity in this situation; I am too much involved emotionally to view it with any calm. Again, I don't think there is the stuff of drama in the situation. To have a conflict in drama you must have a conflict of equals or at least near equals. There is no drama in Rhodesia or South Africa and similarly there is no drama in the North of Ireland. In a lengthy address I gave about the Theatre of Hope and Despair [see above, pp. 15–24], I made the point that American and European plays were nihilistic and concerned with the destruction of man's psyche. But I don't think this is true any longer. Many of the young English dramatists are vitally concerned with resurgent and hopeful man. I think the Theatre of Hope exists in this sense. Writers like Osborne, Wesker and [Henry] Livings are optimistic people who happen to use black canvases. When you discuss the theatre in Ireland you talk of O'Casey and the discussion ends. But the world has become much smaller and we should now view ourselves not in an insular but in a world context. An Irish dramatist need not handle his material differently. The canvas can be as small as you wish, but the more accurately you write and the more truthful you are the more validity your play will have for the world.

It was Lady Gregory who said of the Abbey Theatre's tour of America that the Abbey had won much praise for itself and raised the dignity of Ireland.[1] What the Abbey achieved in its early years was enormous; today its role must change. It cannot keep doing the same thing year after year, decade after decade. What it must now do is what the English National Theatre and any first-rate repertory can do – put on the plays of the country. The Abbey has a measure of financial security in its subsidies and can take risks as no commercial management can. This should be its new strength, and no one should expect it to do today what it did at its inauguration. It is a strange situation in which the Abbey's proud boast is that it plays to ninety-five per cent houses. That is the kind of boast the Windmill Theatre might have made. A better claim would be that they have put on ten plays, nine of which were terrible but one of which was good. The Abbey directors rejected my play *The Mundy Scheme* by three votes to one. When I submitted the play I stipulated that if it were accepted for production I would require Donal Donnelly as director and Godfrey Quigley to play the leading role of the Taoiseach. I asked for a decision within one week. Let me say that I submitted the play with the gravest misgivings and little enthusiasm. One week later Alan Simpson, who was the Abbey's Artistic Adviser, rang Donal Donnelly to say that the play had been rejected.[2] I was not disillusioned. I have never seen myself writing for any particular theatre group or any particular actor or director. When I have written a play I look for the best possible interpretation from a director and actors, and after that my responsibility ends.

I am uneasy about the future of the writer in Ireland. Ireland is becoming a shabby imitation of a third-rate American state. This is what *The Mundy Scheme* is about. We are rapidly losing our identity as a people and because of this that special quality an Irish writer should have will be lost. A writer is the voice of his people and if the people are no longer individuals I cannot see that the writer will have much currency. We are losing the specific national identity which has not been lost by the Dutch or the Belgians or the French or Italians. We are no longer even West Britons; we are East Americans. A writer cannot exist financially in Ireland unless his work is read or performed in Europe or America. An Irish writer can, of course, write serials for television or radio, but I think we would be as well off working in a solicitor's office.

I abandoned short-story writing before I grew tired of it and now that I am becoming disenchanted with the theatre the chances are that I will go back to writing stories. Walter Macken once said to me that he had taken to novel writing because there were too many middlemen in the theatre. All theatre is a kind of compromise. When you write a play you have the ideal actors in mind, but you never get them; you have the ideal director in mind, but you never get him. In one way the Irish writer works under difficult conditions because of our damned Gaelic introspection. In another way he works under better conditions than if he were living in Paris, London or New York. If you write a mediocre play in Dublin you will get it staged and it will be staged reasonably well and receive a responsible reaction. If you write a mediocre play in a big city [abroad] the chances of having it staged are minimal. But if a young Dubliner writes a play it will be seen, and isn't this what he wants? Unfortunately, we look at this little island, which is so tiny, and imagine that the people who live ten streets away are different to ourselves. We are obsessed with ourselves and cannot see ourselves in a global context. One of our great misconceptions is that Ireland can be ruled only by its government and that the best government is composed of businessmen. This is a fallacy. I see no reason why Ireland should not be ruled by its poets and dramatists. Tyrone Guthrie has said that if Yeats and Lady Gregory were alive today they would be unimportant people. This is the way it is going to be, I am afraid.

Plays Peasant and Unpeasant (1972)

It is time we dropped from the calendar of Irish dramatic saints all those playwrights from Farquhar to Shaw – and that includes Steele, Sheridan, Goldsmith and Wilde – who no more belong to the Irish drama than John Field belongs to Irish music or Francis Bacon to Irish painting. Fine dramatists they were, each assured of at least a generous footnote in the history of English drama. But if we take as our definition of Irish drama plays written in Irish or English on Irish subjects and performed by Irishmen, we must scrap all those men who wrote within the English tradition, for the English stage and for the English people, and we can go back no further than 1899, to the night of 8 May, the opening night of the Irish Literary Theatre.

Irish drama is a horse of an altogether different colour and is remarkable for four things. It is only seventy-three years old. It was founded by Yeats, an élitist, who set out to establish an 'unpopular theatre and an audience like a secret society where admission is by favour and never to many', and who discovered with dismay that instead 'we have been the first to create a true People's Theatre . . . . Yet we did not set out to create this sort of theatre and its success has been to me a discouragement and a defeat.'[1] It has produced two playwrights, Synge and O'Casey, who are considered classics. And it has packed into its brief life more riots than the English theatre has seen in eight hundred years.

The Abbey has had almost a monopoly of the riots, ever since the night in 1899 when the Irish Literary Theatre put on *The Countess Cathleen*, right up to last year when a revue, *A State of Chassis*,[2] was physically interrupted by a section of the audience. The revue was shouted down by the objectors who claimed that it 'trivialized' the struggle in Northern Ireland, and television cameras were conveniently at hand at the request of the objectors.

Another interesting aspect of that event is that one of the demon-strators, Lelia Doolan, has since become artistic director of the Abbey, a happy, un-Irish rioter-to-ruler tale.

But it must be admitted that theatre riots are not what they were in Synge's or O'Casey's early days when actors had to have police protection. Indeed, a scholarly study of 'Riots in the Irish Theatre' or, better still, 'The Decline of the Riot in Irish Theatre', would reveal an interesting shift in the attitude of the Irish people to the art of drama, and perhaps a matching decline in the art itself. It would show that in the first quarter of the century we brought to the theatre a high seriousness as worthy in its own way as the seriousness of the playwrights; that we recognized then that the theatre was an important social element that not only reflected but shaped the society it served; that dramatists were revolution-ary in the broadest sense of that word; and that subjective truth – the artist's truth – was dangerously independent of Church and State. Admittedly, there are subtler methods of expressing strong disagreement than spitting on your author and hurling chairs at your players (we learned the more sophisticated art of Church and State censorship later). But the robust technique was at least an indication of a rude involvement, and was certainly the most con-venient and most natural weapon for a peasant society. Because beneath the patina of Hiltonesque hotels and intercontinental jet airports and mohair suits and private swimming pools, that is what we still are – a peasant people.

Peasant is an emotive word. It evokes sympathy (saint, dreamer, pure, individual, pastoral) or disgust (ignorant, vulgar, philistine, thick). But to understand anything about the history or present health of Irish drama, one must first acknowledge the peasant mind, then recognize its two dominant elements: one is a passion for the land; the other a paranoiac individualism. And these two elements have not only been the themes of dozens of Irish plays but have informed in a much wider sense the entire corpus of Irish dramatic work. What O'Faolain said twenty-five years ago is still valid:

> We have always feared towns. We have felt them as spear-heads of life-ways which are complex, troublesome and chal-lenging. Today we call those life-ways 'foreign' and in trying

to impose a peasant life-way on the towns we try to exclude anything which the peasant (especially the Catholic peasant) does not understand.[3]

And again:

The greatest curse of Ireland . . . has been the exaggeration of Irish virtue – our stubbornness, conservatism, enormous arrogance, our power of resistance, our capacity for taking punishment, our laughter, endurance, fatalism, devotion to the past, all taken to that point where every human quality can become a vice instead of a virtue.

I am not suggesting that today's Irish dramatists are mere village entertainers or nationalistic hacks; nor that we are either *engagé* or propagandist. What I am suggesting is that in each of us the line between the Irish mind and the creative mind is much too fine. That there must be a far greater distinction between the Irishman who suffers and the artist's mind which creates.[4] That the intensity of the emotion we all feel for our country (and in the present climate that emotion is heightened) is not of itself the surest foundation for the best drama, which, as Eliot says, comes from 'the intensity of the artistic process, the pressure, so to speak, under which the fusion takes place.'[5]

Perhaps because it is a vulgar art form and more directly dependent on the public than is poetry or music or the visual arts, the theatre has always been more susceptible to outside pressures. And the persistent cry in Ireland at the moment is for a more 'relevant' drama. Write of Ireland today, the critics scream. Show us the vodka-and-tonic society. Show us permissive Dublin. Forget about thatched cottages and soggy fields and emigration. We want the now Ireland. The demand is interesting. Leaving aside the confusion between the art of the writer and the craft of the commentator, it is interesting because it is not a genuine demand for the revelation of a new 'truth' about the country but for a confirmation of a false assumption.

The assumption is that Dublin is a miniature New York, London, Paris, Tokyo, and that it shares with those capitals identical social, economic, moral and cultural problems. And the postulate implies that if the artists would only concoct plays about drug addiction and high-rise apartments and urban aggression and gay power then Dublin's place among the global capitals would be miraculously and publicly assured. The dramatists laugh at this demand because they see how spurious it is: live tail, get dog.

But what the critics are not shouting for and what may well be worthy of the dramatist's probe is the deep schizophrenia of that city, because it is there, and only there, that the urban man and the rural man meet and attempt to mingle. It is this confluence that gives the city its distinctive flavour – visitors call it 'fascination' – the co-existence of Chase Manhattan money with bomb-throwing chauvinism, of land speculation (always land!) with rosary crusades, of Torremolinos package holidays with dole queues, of the necessary intimacy of slum-dwelling with the intense privacy of the countryman. There is no 'victory' for either side because neither side can retain its purity. But I feel that the conflict and mutual change should ignite a dramatic instinct.

Any look at Irish theatre must include a glance at the Gate. The Gate venture was noble. It was founded by Hilton Edwards and Micheál Mac Liammóir as an experimental repertory theatre that devoted itself to the production of highly stylized experimental drama by European, American and Irish playwrights and to the revival of Greek and Shakespearean classics. (The year was 1928, significantly the same year that the Abbey rejected *The Silver Tassie.*) The leavening influence of these productions by the country's two most distinguished men of the theatre cannot be overestimated. If we had not had them, we might never have had Denis Johnston, Austin Clarke's Lyric Theatre, Donagh McDonagh and Brendan Behan. The Abbey still goes on offering Boucicault. But because of Edwards and Mac Liammóir Irish audiences laugh tolerantly, whether at the play or the Abbey directors does not really matter much.

What the future of Irish drama will be must depend on the slow process of development of the Irish mind, and it will shape and be shaped by political events. (In this essay I am not concerned with buildings and subsidies. In Dublin two theatres, the Abbey and the Gate, receive almost adequate state funds. The Abbey has an artistic policy. The Gate had, when Edwards and Mac Liammóir were active there. Another national theatre company is to be formed this year. Its only cultural directive is the curt command:

Tour![6] In Belfast the Lyric [Players Theatre] is kept alive by Arts Council money.)

And it is no help to the Irish dramatist to look outside Ireland, because his situation is substantially different from the French or English or German or American dramatist. Playwrights in other countries carry on or adjust or revolt against the rich tradition they are heirs to. Their function is to illuminate the condition of their people, as they see it, in forms that are determined to a large extent by that condition. Hence Artaud, Peter Brook, Roger Planchon, Brecht, theatre of the absurd, happenings, theatre of fact, tactile theatre, epic theatre, black theatre, etc., etc. Hence, indeed, the lesser concern with *where* theatre can best and most effectively be realized: in a box stage, open stage, thrust stage, in factories, warehouses, canteens, clubs, on the streets. None of these concerns has ever touched us. Not, I think in this case, another example of our in-looking, but simply because we are still too busy with beginnings. Matter is our concern, not form.

In a recent newspaper article, Benedict Kiely, commenting on the work of John McGahern and Edna O'Brien, said that until they appeared

> no Irish writer that I can think of ever spoke to the young. In terms of patriotism, yes, and the rising of the moon, and did that play of mine send out certain men the English shot. But not about domestic matters like masturbation around which the adults and the ages had built a theology and a mythology, or the passing or failing of examinations, or the domination of a strong father, or a mother dying slowly of a dread disease, or of young girls wondering what it was all about and being determined to find out.

Apart from the fact that the claim is dubious and brutal as a summary of the fictional themes of Mr McGahern and Miss O'Brien, it is remarkable that Mr Kiely should list these topics as major concerns of the young or of artists. It reads like an advertisement for strong, human-interest, half-hour television plays. Happily we are not as far behind the scratch line as that. If we were, the International Theatre Festival in Dublin would be an event to be avoided.

So what of the future? It looks as if the slow process will be severely jolted. It requires no gift of prophecy to foresee that the revolt in Northern Ireland is going to spread to the Republic; and if you believe that art is an instrument of the revolutionary process, then you can look forward to a spate of committed plays. I do not believe that art is a servant of any movement. But during the period of unrest I can foresee that the two allegiances that have bound the Irish imagination – loyalty to the most authoritarian church in the world and devotion to a romantic ideal we call Kathleen – will be radically altered. Faith and Fatherland: new definitions will be forged, and then new loyalties, and then new social groupings. It will be a bloody process. And when it has subsided, the Irish imagination – that vivid, slovenly, anarchic, petulant, alert to the eternal, impatient with the here and now instrument – will have to set about shaping and interpreting the new structure in art forms.

Meanwhile, in Germany [Rolf] Hochhuth writes surrealistic documentaries about human responsibility. In England Edward Bond writes about the violent self-destruction of mankind. In France [Roger] Planchon celebrates change in all its forms. In America Edward Albee writes of the impossibility of human communication. And in Ireland, as I write this, in the capital's three largest theatres, [Dion] Boucicault capers on the Abbey stage, Cinderella on the Olympia, Robin Hood on the Gaiety. Some enterprising impresario should book Nero and his fiddle for a long Irish season.

In Interview with Eavan Boland (1973)

I interviewed Brian Friel in 1970 at his home six miles south of the Derry–Donegal border, looking across the expanse of the Foyle. He spoke then of the difficulty of finding a theme; as I was leaving he handed me a new novel to read by an American poet, James Dickey, called *Deliverance*. I knew of Dickey as a respected, ironic artist, very far from a household name. Two years later and some months *Deliverance* has become a film, grossing almost as much as *The Godfather*, and Brian Friel has found a theme.

When *The Freedom of the City* goes on the Abbey stage, and very shortly afterwards appears at the Royal Court in England, he is prepared for a certain amount of misinterpretation by his audience. Already it has been suggested that the play is about Bloody Sunday, but, as he explains, it is not:

> It's not about Bloody Sunday. In fact, the play began long before Bloody Sunday happened. I was working on this theme for about ten months before Bloody Sunday. And then Bloody Sunday happened, and the play I was writing, and wasn't succeeding with, suddenly found a focus. I was stuck until this point, and this was a kind of clarification. The play, in fact, is the story of three people who are on a Civil Rights march in Derry city in 1970. The march finishes in the Guild Hall Square. There's a public meeting. Then the British Army moves in, breaks up the meeting and these three people take refuge in the Guild Hall and find themselves in the Mayor's parlour.

At first glance, *The Freedom of the City* provides the scenario of a political play, even from Friel's brief outline of it. Yet it would be surprising if it was. There has never been anything of the polemicist or the propagandist in his work, with the possible exception of *The Mundy Scheme* [1969] which he now dismisses as 'bad just because it wasn't half good enough'.

In fact, far from being concerned with the impersonal decisions which affect life, Friel is obsessed with the personal, interior world of self-deception which only comes to light in crisis, if ever. For example, the insight which Cass McGuire has into her life comes only when she is confronted at the end of it with the ruin of her illusions; similarly in 'Foundry House', one of the finest short stories Friel has written, the nun in America [*sic*, for Africa] who maintains an illusory sense of her family's fortunes long after they have declined, is far more indicative of the concerns of Friel's work than any political stance could be.[1] He is an artist preoccupied with the individual and his cryptic humiliations, rather than with the public gesture, as, for example, John Arden is.

An indication of how independent his work is of the moment, the political watershed, can be assessed by the fact that *The Freedom of the City* began as a play set in the eighteenth century and was constructed around evictions. At that time it was titled *John Butt's Bothy*. Though that plot and place have disappeared, Friel still regards his new play, like its embryo, as being a study of poverty.

One of the things that makes him wary of reaction to *The Freedom of the City* is the aesthetic worry about how near an artist can afford to be to his subject:

> This play raises the old problem of writing about events which are still happening. It's the old problem of the distinction between the mind that suffers and the man who creates.[2] The trouble about this particular play in many ways is that people are going to find something immediate in it, some kind of reportage. And I don't think that's in it at all. Very often an accident in history will bring about a meeting-point, a kind of fusion for you. And this is what happened. This is a play which is about poverty. But because we're all involved in the present situation people are going to say 'this is a very unfair play'. And of necessity it has got to be unfair in this public kind of way. I hope that people will come to see this with an open mind. But, of course, they may come and see in it only a confirmation of some kind of prejudice in the play anyhow.

Friel's emphasis on the chasm between the mind that suffers and the man who creates proves two things: one of them is simply that he has read Eliot's influential essay, which draws that distinction; secondly, that he is a prey to the confusion that an essentially private, scrupulously honest artist must feel living next door to a public, uproariously violent situation. Because he is a private artist, the abundance of themes that the violence seems to offer means little to him as a writer, however much it may affect him as a man. Therefore, the focus of *The Freedom of the City* is simply applicable to that play, and represents no new, rich seam which he can work: 'I don't think it's a breakthrough. I would love to think it was. But life's not as easy as that.'

In this way he describes his dilemma as a playwright. As a person, naturally enough, he is as bewildered as anyone by the continuing horror of the situation in the city where he was born [*sic*], and in which he grew up. But he evidently does not look to that situation to provide him with achievements and insights in art. When I asked him what his deep objectives were as a writer, he was, understandably, to use his own word, circuitous. 'I suppose I want some kind of definitive statement that would give myself some kind of clarification. Yet what that statement would be about I don't know. If I did that would be the whole answer.'

Friel is far happier talking about the machinery of theatre than about the meaning of his contribution to it. He sees a crisis in theatre that is not peculiar to Ireland:

> All over the English-speaking world theatre is in a state of chaos. And in this country, where we don't have a theatrical tradition, we don't know whether we should attend theatre, or go and be entertained by it, or go as a kind of package tour to it. This may be the fault of directors or the writers. In any case, it exists.

From everything that Friel has said, those who go to *The Freedom of the City* expecting to find a resolution to the violence of the North, or an insight into the spirit of Derry, are likely to be disappointed. Naturally, this is so, since they would be searching through a play for what is more properly the province of a White Paper or a Ministerial directive. If, however, they go looking for a subtle increase and expansion of a playwright's skills and concerns they will think the experience worthwhile. The plot of the play should whet the appetite, but if it satisfied it then one would feel Friel had fallen for the bait of reportage rather than art. He is unlikely to do that, for he has served one of the most exacting apprenticeships in Irish writing, having known the rejections of his work – as, for instance, of *Philadelphia, Here I Come!* by the Abbey, and *The Mundy Scheme* by the New York critics – as well as a great deal of success.[3]

Currently he is working on a new play. But it is at so early a stage in its development that he is unwilling to talk about it. In a few months he is going to America to see *Crystal and Fox* being performed there. Finally, he has this to say about writing about Northern events; it could serve as a caveat to other writers who draw too freely on the present situation:

> The trouble with Derry at the moment is that there is an articulation there, but it's a kind of cliché articulation, because everybody is so obsessed with the media and what has happened yesterday that we have all got answers for everything.

However Friel, the Derry citizen, may respond Friel the artist is likely to continue feeling he has an answer to few things, and that those answers he has are suspect. In this time of ready remedies it is a welcome stance.

In Interview with Fachtna O'Kelly (1975)

When playwright Brian Friel's new *magnum opus*, *Volunteers*, opened in the Abbey Theatre, Dublin, earlier this month it was received with almost universal put-downs by the critics of the national newspapers.

One notice said that 'as a realistic play it is mildly amusing'. Another said it was a humbling experience for such a fine writer as Friel and, for the Abbey, another misjudgment, while a third critic concluded his review by asking, 'Your point, Mr Friel – your point?'

Hardly a very flattering series of notices. And it would seem that they have had some effect on the Abbey's box office, for seat occupancy, as the term goes, is hovering around the 50 per cent mark, about 25 per cent down on the yearly average.

Once again, the reviews raised the whole question of the role of the theatre critic, the effect of notices on attendances and the contribution that they can make to the existence of 'live' theatre in Ireland.

As far as Mr Friel is concerned, the critic can be one of two things. 'He or she may be a kind of litmus paper, so perfectly attuned to popular taste that they can actually reflect it. Or the critic can, over a period of time or through the quality of stuff written, build up a certain amount of respect and a worthwhile and deserved reputation. I believe that we have an abundance of the first kind in Ireland but, I think, a lack of the latter.'

In the case of *Volunteers*, Mr Friel points out that the critics did not write anything different from what they had said in the past. 'They were possibly a bit more obtuse than usual' is as much as he will say.

The effect of bad notices can be twofold, he believes. They may firstly put an audience completely off going to a play, or, secondly, they could mean that people would attend a play but in a conditioned rather than an open frame of mind.

61

'But more important than its effect on attendances is the fact that a barrage of bad notices can very often submerge a play for three or four years. It often takes that long for a real opinion to emerge. And it also means that foreign theatres will be slow to put on a work which has been poorly received by the critics in Ireland,' he adds.

Obviously, he is of the opinion that theatrical criticism in Ireland is not all that it should be. He believes, however, that the fault lies not with the individuals involved but with the newspaper managements.

'For instance, I don't see any point in sending a man to review a play when he has been working for the rest of the week on news stories. It is inevitable that his attitude will be affected by a kind of news-story consciousness.'

Newspapers would have to search around for the best possible person and the one whose opinions were not being trivialized by the rest of his work. The assessment of a theatrical experience was, of course, a particular craft and one that needed a mind free of other attitudes.

'In the end, the responsibility lies with the newspaper managements. They must ensure that the critics they appoint are not also expected to report on things like weddings or other news events. Either that, or the reviews must be done by a complete outsider.'

Critics, indeed, can help the playwright considerably and he instances the case of [George Jean] Nathan, who had been of very considerable assistance to Sean O'Casey in the formation of his plays.

As for himself, Mr Friel adds, he does not pay that much attention to notices written by the theatre critics. 'I read them, certainly, and I observe what they are saying. But they certainly don't affect me personally.'

Extracts from a Sporadic Diary
(1976–78): *Aristocrats*

31 August 1976

Back from holidays and now stancing myself towards winter and work. Throughout the summer there were faint signals of a very long, very slow-moving, very verbose play; a family saga of three generations; articulate people wondering about themselves and ferreting into concepts of Irishness. Religion, politics, money, position, marriages, revolts, affairs, love, loyalty, disaffection.

Would it be a method of writing to induce a flatness, a quiet, an emptiness, and then to work like a farm-labourer out of that dull passivity?

1 September 1976

A. B. describes C. B.'s new play to me as 'a romp'. A curious phrase, attempting to disarm. This is merely to make you laugh, it suggests; the artist is on Sabbatical; the man like yourselves is At Home to you; drop in for the crack.

This is precisely what we can't do. We cannot split ourselves in this way. We must synthesize in ourselves all those uneasy elements – father, lover, breadwinner, public man, private man – so that they constitute the determining artist. But if we attempt to give one element its head, what we do is bleed the artist in us of a necessary constituent, pander to an erratic appetite within us. The play that is visiting me brings with it each time an odour of musk – incipient decay, an era wilted, people confused and nervous. If there are politics they are underground.

10 September 1976

Somehow relevant to the play – Mailer on his daughters: 'If he did something wrong, they being women would grow up around the mistake and somehow convert it to knowledge. But his sons! He had the feeling that because they were men their egos were more fragile – a serious error might hurt them for ever.'

17 September 1976

A dozen false starts. And the trouble with false starts is that once they are attempted, written down, they tend to become actual, blood-related to the whole. So that finally each false start will have to be dealt with, adjusted, absorbed. Like life.

30 September 1976

Coming back to the idea of the saga-drama, maybe even a trilogy with the Clydesdale pace and rhythm of O'Neill. Possibly. Intimidating.

3 November 1976

For some months now there is a single, recurring image: a very plain-looking girl of about thirty-eight – perhaps slightly masculine in her mannerisms – wheels on to the stage her mother in a wheelchair. Her father follows docilely, like a tinker's pony.

7 November 1976

I think I've got a scent of the new play. Scarcely any idea of character, plot, movement, scene; but a definite whiff of the atmosphere the play will exude. Something stirring in the undergrowth. At the moment I don't want to stalk what may be stirring there. No. I will sit still and wait. It will move again. And then again. And each time its smell will become more distinct. And then finally when that atmosphere is confident and distinctive, I and the play will move towards one another and inhabit that atmosphere.

27 November 1976

'You have chosen to be what you are' – Sartre.

7 December 1976

The crux with the new play arises – as usual with me – with its form. Whether to reveal slowly and painstakingly and with almost realized tedium the workings of the family; or with some kind of supra-realism, epiphanies, in some way to make real the essences of these men and women by sidestepping or leaping across the boredom of their small talk, their trivial chatterings, etc. etc. But I suppose the answer to this will reveal itself when I know/possess the play. Now I am only laying siege to it.

10 December 1976

THE CANARY IN THE MINE-SHAFT. Title? (It is important when its song hesitates and stops.)

15 December 1976

A persistent sense that the play is about three aging sisters. And a suspicion that its true direction is being thwarted by irrelevant politics, social issues, class. And an intuition that implicit in their language, attitudes, style, will be all the 'politics' I need. Concentrate on the three girls. Maybe another married sister who visits with her husband. Maybe set some years back – just pre-war?

17 December 1976

Endless and disturbed wanderings in various directions, with considerations of masks, verse, expressionism, etc. etc. But the one constant is Judith who is holding on to late young-womanhood, who has brothers and sisters, and who misses/has nursed an old father. THE JUDAS HOLE?

O'Neill: '. . . but O'Casey is an artist and the soap-box [is] no place for his great talent. The hell of it seems to be, when an artist starts saving the world, he starts losing himself. I know, having been bitten by the salvationist bug myself at times. But only momentarily . . .'[1]

28 December 1976

Judith-Alice-Claire; and Father.

7 January 1977

Making no headway with the new play; apart, perhaps, from the suitability of the word 'consternation' to our lives. I feel – again – that the intrusion of active politics is foreign to the hopes and sensibilities of the people who populate this play.

8 January 1977

The play – this must be remembered, reiterated, constantly pushed into the centre of the stage – is about *family life*, its quality, its cohesion, its stultifying effects, its affording of opportunities for what we designate 'love' and 'affection' and 'loyalty'. Class, politics, social aspiration are the qualifying décor but not the core.

10 January 1977

Going back over four months of notes for the new play and find that the only residue left by dozens of strained excursions is: an aging, single woman; a large house for which she acts as medium; a baby-alarm; the word 'consternation'; and perhaps various house furnishings that are coyly referred to as Yeats, O'Casey, Chesterton, etc. Cryptic symbols that may contain rich and comprehensive revelations – or disparate words that have no common sympathy? So all I can do is handle and feel them. Talk with them.

25 January 1977

Every day I visit the site where the materials of the new play lie covered under Cellophane sheets. I have no idea of its shape from those outlines. I can envisage what the final structure may be. But I have no plans, no drawings – only tempting and illusory 'artist's impressions'.

31 January 1977

Is there an anti-art element in theatre in that it doesn't speak to the individual in his absolute privacy and isolation but addresses him as an audience? And if it is possible to receive the dramatist and apprehend him as an individual, is the art being confronted on a level that wasn't intended?

2 May 1977

Mark time. Mark time. Pursue the commonplace. Tag on to the end of the ritualistic procession.

24 May 1977

The play has become elaborate, like a presentation Easter egg. Has it a centre?

25 May 1977

A persistent feeling that I should leave the play aside until it finds its own body and substance. Stop hounding it. Crouch down. Wait. Listen. In its own time it may call out.

26 May 1977

To see the thing exactly as it is and then to create it anew.

2 June 1977

What makes Chekhov accessible to so many different people for 180 years is his suggestion of sadness, of familiar melancholy, despite his false/cunning designation 'Comedies'. Because sadness and melancholy are finally reassuring. Tragedy is not reassuring. Tragedy demands completion. Chekhov was afraid to face completion.

21 June 1977

My attitude to the new play alternates between modest hope and total despair. What I seem to be unable to do is isolate its essence from the faltering existence I keep trying to impose on it. I keep shaping characters, looking for modes of realization, investing forms – when what I need to do is determine what the core of the play is and where it lies.

10 September 1977

I have a sense that everyone (i.e. all the characters) is ready in the wings, waiting to move on stage; but somehow something isn't quite right on the set. So they drift about, smoking, scarcely talking to one another, encased in privacy. A sense, too, that that slight adjustment, if only I knew what it was, could endow them all with articulacy. Maybe that's the essence of the play: the burden of the incommunicable.

17 September 1977

Six days at THE JUDAS HOLE, when it seemed to take off, not with a dramatic lift, but resolutely, efficiently. And now at a standstill – that total immobility when it is not a question of a scene stuttering and dying but when the entire play seems specious, forced, concocted. Trying to inflate and make buoyant something that is riddled with holes.

18 September 1977

Moving, inching forward again. But whole areas – central characters, integral situations – about which I know nothing. And my ignorance and their magnitude looming and threatening.

26 September 1977

The play has stopped; has thwarted me. I still work at it. But it sulks. And yet – and yet I sense its power. If only I could seduce it past its/my blockage.

17 October 1977

The imagination is the only conscience.

11 November 1977

On a day (days? weeks! months!) like this when I come upstairs at a fixed time and sit at this desk for a certain number of hours, without a hope of writing a line, without a creative thought in my head, I tell myself that what I am doing is making myself obediently available – patient, deferential, humble. A conceit? Whether or not, it's all I can do.

13 December 1977

'Sometimes, however, to be a "ruined" man is itself a vocation' – Eliot on Coleridge.

16 December 1977

The dramatist has to recycle his experience through the pressure-chamber of his imagination. He has then to present this new reality to a public – 300 diverse imaginations come together with no more serious intent than the casual wish to be 'entertained'. And he has got to forge those 300 imaginations into one perceiving faculty, dominate and condition them so that they become attuned to the tonality of the transmission and consequently to its meaning. Because if a common keynote isn't struck and agreed on, the receiving institutions remain dissipated and unreceptive. But to talk of 'meaning' is inaccurate. We say 'What is the play about?' with more accuracy than 'What does the play mean?' Because we don't go to art for meaning. We go to it for perceptions of new adjustments and new arrangements.

1 February 1978

Yesterday I finally browbeat the material into Act 1. There may be value in it. I don't know. Occasionally I get excited by little portions. Do they add up to anything?

19 May 1978

The play completed and christened ARISTOCRATS.

In Interview with Elgy Gillespie (1978)

Northerner Brian Friel has written some vastly different plays since *Philadelphia, Here I Come!* and that must in part be due to the way times have vastly changed. Many people feel that his is still the strongest and most original voice of Irish theatre, and that his plays need to be reappraised at intervals to be seen in shifting contexts. His last play was *Living Quarters* at the Abbey [1977]. He is working on his newest play at home in Donegal and the thought of renouncing stage-writing, he says, never enters his head.

'I detect no signs of either a theatre revival or a theatre decline in the North. In Belfast the Lyric continues as usual and the Arts Theatre has been reopened. Coleraine has got the new Riverside and Derry hopes to have a new theatre with a permanent company in a few years. Maybe this all adds up to a revival. I don't know. The proliferation of theatre buildings is no yardstick. It is what takes place in them that is important.

'For example, over the past fifteen years in the USA, civic-minded people right across the country have been possessed by a frenzy to build theatres and arts centres. These elegant and expensive buildings now exist. But a theatre revival? I see no sign of one.

'Nor can I explain why young writers are not attracted to the theatre here. Artists in this country always seem to have found the novel and poetry and the short story more satisfying forms. (And even though playwrights are frequently reminded that we aspire to poetry, Eliot believed that "the majority, perhaps, certainly a large number, of poets hanker for the stage".[1])

'Perhaps the complicated organization and trappings of the theatre frighten the young writer off. Perhaps the acquisition of the necessary craft. Perhaps the fact that the work can be realized only through actors ("the intervention of performers" is Eliot's revealing phrase, suggesting that he believed drama closer to literature than to the theatre[2]). Perhaps the whiff of the market-place.

Perhaps – particularly in this country – the total lack of an informed critical response. Perhaps – again something peculiar to this country – the blurring of the distinction between professional and amateur theatre, a confusion that tends to diminish both the seriousness of professional theatre and the parish values of the amateur theatre.'

Elgy Gillespie: What about politics?
Brian Friel: . . . You go on to talk about the new group of young English writers – Brenton, Bond, Hare – and ask, 'Why can't people of that sort write here?'

We are on firmer ground here. All the young men you mention are committed to the left, some of them professed revolutionaries, who look to the theatre as a pulpit because they believe that it is the legitimate, and perhaps only, function of theatre to change the political face of the world.

Ireland does not seem to infuse her writers with that kind of political zeal. Or to put it another way: Irishmen and women with that kind of vision and commitment find modes other than the arts through which to express themselves. Of course, we have had and will have plays and novels and poetry and short stories that can be called 'political'. But where we differ from the English playwrights you mention is, I suggest, that we don't think of ourselves as politicians, nor do we consider politics our commitment.

There was a time when I would have agreed that, given certain conditions, great playwrights could be nurtured. And I would have pointed to the Moscow Art Theatre – Chekhov, and to the Provincetown Players – O'Neill, and to the Abbey – Synge. But the older I get, the more sceptical I am of this thesis.

I still believe that you can have the happy concurrence of the man and the moment, when a great dramatist's capabilities are a product of, and in return generate, a period of distinctive intellectual ferment. But the moment alone does not make the man, nor the man the moment.
EG: And now?
BF: My present view is more stern. Financial assistance is helpful. Competent actors in a well-equipped theatre are helpful. The existence of a well-informed critical atmosphere is helpful. But in the end not one of these things alone will make a dramatist. He

appears. The very most we can do is make his birth and growth less uncomfortable.

Ever since the Greeks, there have been long periods when theatre went into decline, became submerged, surfaced again. I see no sign of such a decline now. But if it were to happen, let it happen.

Extracts from a Sporadic Diary
(1979): *Translations*

(I do not keep a diary. But occasionally, usually when the work
has hit a bad patch, I make sporadic notes, partly as a discipline to
keep me at the desk, partly in the wan hope that the casual jot-
tings will induce something better. These notes were made
throughout 1979. I was working on a play that came to be called
Translations. *Translations* is set in a hedge-school in Ballybeg,
County Donegal. The year is 1833. The British army is engaged in
mapping the whole of Ireland, a process which involves the
renaming of every place-name in the country. It is a time of great
upheaval for the people of Ballybeg: their hedge-school is to be
replaced by one of the new national schools; there is recurring
potato blight; they have to acquire a new language (English); and
because their townland is being renamed, everything that was
familiar is becoming strange.)

1 May 1979

Mayday. Snowing. Still circling around the notion of the hedge-
school/ordnance survey play. Reluctant to touch down, to make
the commitment of beginning.

11 May 1979

Bits and pieces of the new play are coming together. Characters
are acquiring form and voice. Attitudes are finding shape and
tongue. But only on this very basic level are there the first stirrings. The bigger issues – what the image of map-making evokes,
what the play was born of and where it hopes to go to – none of
these is acquiring definition. But at this point one still hopes for
the numinous.

14 May 1979

Went to Urris today, the setting of the hedge-school in the play-in-the-head. No response to the place apart from some sense of how the ordinary British sappers might have reacted to this remote, bleak, desolate strip of land attenuated between mountain and sea. And perhaps in an attempt to commit myself to the material I bought a first edition of Colonel Colby's *Memoir of the City and North Western Liberties of Londonderry*.[1]

The people from Urris/Ballybeg would have been Irish-speaking in 1833. So a theatrical conceit will have to be devised by which – even though the actors speak English – the audience will assume or accept that they are speaking Irish. Could that work?

15 May 1979

I keep returning to the same texts: the letters of John O'Donovan, Colby's *Memoir*, *A Paper Landscape* by John Andrews,[2] *The Hedge-Schools of Ireland* by Dowling,[3] Steiner's *After Babel*.[4] And at each rereading I get interested in some trivial detail or subside beneath the tedium of the whole idea. For some reason the material resists the intense and necessary fusion of its disparate parts into one whole, and the intense and necessary mental heat that accomplishes that. One aspect that keeps eluding me: the wholeness, the integrity, of that Gaelic past. Maybe because I don't believe in it.

16 May 1979

I can envisage a few scenes: the hedge-school classroom; the love scene between lovers who have no common language; the actual task of places being named. Nothing more. The play is not extending its influence into unrealized territories. Stopping short at what it says and shows only.

22 May 1979

The thought occurred to me that what I was circling around was a political play and that thought panicked me. But it is a political play – how can that be avoided? If it is not political, what is it? Inaccurate history? Social drama?

23 May 1979

I believe that I am reluctant even to name the characters, maybe because the naming-taming process is what the play is about.

29 May 1979

Reading and rereading Colby and Andrews and O'Donovan and Steiner and Dowling. Over the same territories again and again and again. I am now at the point when the play *must* be begun and yet all I know about it is this:

I don't want to write a play about Irish peasants being suppressed by English sappers.

I don't want to write a threnody on the death of the Irish language.

I don't want to write a play about land-surveying.

Indeed I don't want to write a play about naming places.

And yet portions of all these are relevant. Each is part of the atmosphere in which the real play lurks.

1 June 1979

What worries me about the play – if there is a play – are the necessary peculiarities, especially the political elements. Because the play has to do with language and only language. And if it becomes overwhelmed by that political element, it is lost.

18 June 1979

In Ballybeg, at the point when the play begins, the cultural climate is a dying climate – no longer quickened by its past, about to be plunged almost overnight into an alien future. The victims in this situation are the transitional generation. The old can retreat into and find immunity in the past. The young acquire some facility with the new cultural implements. The in-between ages become lost, wandering around in a strange land. Strays.

22 June 1979

Something finally on paper. But what is on paper is far removed from what I thought the play would deal with. For some time there will be this duality – the actual thing and the ideal thing, neither acknowledging the other. Then at some point they must converge. Or one is lost – and then the play is lost.

25 June 1979

Work on the play at a standstill. A complete power failure. This is always accompanied by a lethargy so total that it seeps into everyday things: all activity collapses. And it is also accompanied by a complete loss of faith in the whole *idea* of the play.

I have never found an antidote to this lethargy. Just drive the work on, mechanically, without belief, vaguely trusting in an instinctive automatic pilot.

2 July 1979

A busy week. The first thirteen pages rewritten a dozen times. To create the appropriate atmosphere. To create each voice and endow it with its appropriate pitch. To indicate the themes that will be inhabited and cultivated and to guide the play carefully towards them. Sheepdog trials.

And now standstill again. Because now that so much is on paper – the characters introduced, their voices distinctive, the direction of the play indicated – everything is so subtly wrong, just so slightly off-key, just so slightly out of focus, that the whole play is flawed. And the difficulty at this stage is to identify those small distortions. Because what the play and the characters and their voices and the themes ought to be – the ideal, the play-in-the-head, the model – can't be known until it is made real. The catch-22 situation. So you rework, go back over notes. And try to keep faith with that instinct. And at the same time you are aware that each day, as each page is forged, faith is being transferred from that nebulous concept in the head to that permanent and imperfect word on the page.

3 July 1979

Complete stop. Are the characters only mouthpieces for certain predetermined concepts? Is the play only an ideas play? And indeed are those ideas amenable to dramatic presentation?

4 July 1979

A persistent sense – the logic of the emotions? – that the character Manus is physically maimed.

6 July 1979

One of the mistakes of the direction in which the play is presently pulling is the almost wholly *public* concern of the theme: how does the eradication of the Irish language and the substitution of English affect this particular *society*? How long can a *society* live without its tongue? Public questions; issues for politicians; and that's what is wrong with the play now. The play must concern itself only with the exploration of the dark and private places of individual souls.

11 September 1979

What is so deceptive and so distressing is that the terrain looks so firm and that I think I know it intimately. But the moment I begin to move across it, the ground gives under me. There are a few solid stepping-stones – some characters fully realized – some scenes complete and efficient – but they exist without relationship to one another.

9 October 1979

Persistent, nose-to-the-desk, 9.30 a.m.–5.30 p.m., grinding work. Two acts completed. About to begin Act 3. Final acts are always less taxing because they are predetermined by what has already happened and at this point each character only completes himself, fulfils himself.

I'm not sure what has been achieved. I am more acutely aware of what has been lost, diluted, confused, perverted than of what has been caught and revealed. A sense, too, that on occasion I have lost faith in the fiction and shouted what should have been overheard. But there is still time.

5 November 1979

The play, named *Translations*, completed.

The task of writing the play, the actual job of putting the pattern together, itself generates belief in the pattern. The act and the artifact sustain one another. And now that the play is finished the value of the pattern and belief in the pattern diminish and lethargy sets in: the life process. But only after the play is produced will I be completely cleansed of my subscription to this particular pattern, this ordering of things. Then a vigour will be summoned. Then a new pattern will have to be forged.

The process seems trivial and transient because the patterns are so impermanent. But is there another way? It is a kind of vigilance – keeping the bush from encroaching into the yard. All art is a diary of evolution; markings that seemed true of and for their time; adjustments in stance and disposition; opening to what seemed the persistence of the moment. Map-makings.

In Interview with Ciaran Carty (1980)

Although set in the days of the hedge-schools – British soldiers are carrying out an ordnance survey to establish English versions of local Irish place names – *Translations* expresses the theme of people living in a language that is not their own as a riveting metaphor for the North's continuing trauma.

Brian Friel, with Belfast actor Stephen Rea, set up their own company Field Day to stage *Translations* and chose Derry for the opening because it embodied the meeting of two cultures: the place became an extension of the play. During the week he has been talking with me about this concept of theatre and about the role of the dramatist in a changing Ireland.

He plops a tea bag into a cup of boiling water. 'I'm used to drinking tea in green-rooms and it's always filthy,' Friel apologizes.

Not that we're in a conventional green-room: the huge first-floor room of the Guildhall, with its high ceiling and panelled walls, has been made available to Field Day for rehearsals by Derry City Council. That Field Day should be in the Guildhall at all – to say nothing of Unionist mayor Marlene Jefferson leading the applause on opening night – is in itself remarkable.

To the minority in the North this intimidating neo-Gothic building overlooking the Foyle has always been a symbol of domination. 'This is theirs, boy, and your very presence here is a sacrilege,' jeered Skinner in Friel's 1973 play *The Freedom of the City*. With two other demonstrators he had taken refuge from CS gas in the Mayor's Parlour when troops broke up a civil rights march. Mistaken for an IRA assault force, they came under fire from the British and were shot as they surrendered. Thus was created a savagely ironic analogy to Bloody Sunday [30 January 1972].

But all that is changing. The Guildhall has fallen to words rather than bullets. Even with the recession biting deep – over

10,000 jobs have been lost in the area – a power-sharing Council offers Derry the beginnings of hope.

Friel's new play is in keeping with this new tolerance. He hasn't written a polemic. Theatre for him has never been a soap-box. His plays explore the ambiguities and confusions that pervade life; the truths of his characters are never more than approximations.

'The play found expression in the issue of actual place names,' he tells me, 'but I think in some way my concern is more with the whole problem that writers in this country experience: having to handle a language that is not native to them. There's a line where the hedge-school teacher says that they'll have to learn these names and they'll have to make them their new home. And in some way that's what the play is about: having to use a language that isn't our own.

'But I'm not talking about the revival of the Irish language. I'm just talking about the language we have now and what use we make of it and about the problems that having it gives us. The assumption, for instance, is that we speak the same language as England. And we don't. The sad irony, of course, is that the whole play is written in English. It ought to be written in Irish.'

Much of the theatrical impact of *Translations* comes from Friel's inspired device of having all the characters speak the same language but with a translator all the time interpreting what the English and the Irish are saying to each other: a recurring reminder of the fundamental differences that can be embodied in the same language.

'Somebody asked me if it had a political message,' says Friel ruefully. 'Well, if it has, I don't know what it is. Of course, the play is also concerned with the English presence here. No matter how benign they may think it has been, finally the presence of any foreigner in your land is malign. Even if the people who were instrumental in bringing it in have the best motives – as some of them had.

'We forget that it was the minority here – to step into that jargon – it was the Catholics who sent for the British troops in the height of the problem. And now the "Brits Out" calls are coming from the same people.'

But politics are merely incidental to Friel's preoccupation with words. Hugh points out in *Translations*: 'it is not the literal past, the "facts" of history, that shape us, but images of the past embodied in language.'

As a playwright Friel has been conditioned by this experience as much as anyone else: perhaps more so. 'It's a problem dramatists here never really faced up to: the problem of writing in the language of another country. We're a very recent breed. Poets and novelists, I think, belong to a less fractured tradition than we do. We've only existed since Synge and Yeats. There was no such thing as an indigenous Irish drama until 1904.

'Before that, dramatists from Ireland always had to write for the English stage: to pitch their voice in an English way. They had to do that if they were to practise their craft. The whole Irish drama tradition from Farquhar to Behan is pitted with writers doing that. Ultimately they were maimed.

'But there's a big change now. What many are doing is writing for ourselves. Not in any insular or parochial sense but they want to be heard by their own people. And if they're overheard by anyone else, that's a bonus.'

But having said that, Friel is at pains not be thought to be making a cult of Irishness. 'John McGahern once told you in an interview that he did not want to be considered as an Irish writer. And I can see the danger in that. But I think it's an appellation that other people put on you. So what the hell. You go and do your job.'

Which is how Field Day came about: to give life to the idea of writing for an Irish audience rather than primarily for Broadway or the West End. The logical follow-through comes after Dublin with a series of one-night stands in Magherafelt, Dungannon, Newry, Carrickmore, Armagh and Enniskillen.

'But we're the most reluctant producers,' Friel laughs. He formed Field Day with Stephen Rea ('The company's name is derived from both our names') because it was the only way to get money from the Northern Ireland Arts Council to perform *Translations*. 'They only fund existing establishments so we had to become an establishment.'

Now they find themselves into something much larger than they had anticipated, having to worry about everything from getting out contracts to putting up 'no smoking' signs. 'It's not like going into the Abbey where everything is provided and all you do is sit in on rehearsals and that's it!'

Even with £40,000 from Belfast, £10,000 from the Dublin Arts Council and £13,000 for a new stage and lighting system in the Guildhall from Derry Council ('their help and enthusiasm have been incredible'), Field Day is unlikely to break even. 'The issue is how small the deficit can be kept to. But the response has been so good that I'm much less worried than I was.

'We haven't given any thought to what's going to happen next. Perhaps the play will go to Hampstead. I'd love to see it performed in Belgium or Montreal or parts of Russia where there's the same problem of two cultures and languages coming together. But that's all romanticizing.'

Friel has lived all his life around Derry. 'We moved here from Omagh when I was ten. My father was a teacher and I became a teacher too, but gave it up to write stories for *The New Yorker*. They paid such enormous money I found I could live off three stories a year.'

Tyrone Guthrie invited him out to Minneapolis to the first of the regional theatres he had started. 'I don't know what I learned there but I suppose it was some smell of what theatre was about.'

Out of the experience came *Philadelphia, Here I Come!* in 1964, which became the longest-running Irish play on Broadway, a record not surpassed until last year's triumph of Hugh Leonard's *Da*.

Since then he has had play after play on Broadway – *The Loves of Cass McGuire, Lovers, The Mundy Scheme, The Freedom of the City, Faith Healer* – yet international success has failed to lure him away from the North. He continues to live with his wife Anne and five children a couple of miles over the Border in Muff, County Donegal.

Which is not really surprising. All his plays are set in Ireland and rooted in the Irish experience: that is where his material is.

Friel's plays give universal form to the particularities of his experience: the way he finds to express an idea invariably becomes an extension of that idea. 'The crux with a new play arises with its form,' he says. Thus *Philadelphia* has two actors to personify Gar's inner and outer selves. *Faith Healer* consists entirely of monologues, emphasizing the separateness of the characters. *Translations* is rooted in the varying nuances inherent in the same language on different tongues.

'A play offers you a shape and a form to accommodate your

anxieties and disturbances in that period of life you happen to be passing through', he explains. 'But you outgrow that and you change and grope for a new shape and a new articulation of it, don't you?'

He boils another kettle, to all appearances like a tweed-jacketed teacher in some school common room. Derry is full of his former pupils, to whom he's known by the nickname Scobie.

He is a meticulous craftsman, attending every rehearsal, never letting go of a play until it is a reality on the stage. 'The dramatist ought to be able to exercise complete control over the realization of his characters. The director can bring an objective view to the script that a writer can't have. But I'm very doubtful about the whole idea of a director interpreting a play in any kind of way that's distinctive to him.

'A good director homes in on the core of what a play is about and realizes that and becomes self-effacing in the process. A director is like the conductor of an orchestra and the actors are the musicians. They are all there to play the score as it is written.'

If that makes Friel a conventional playwright, he's not bothered. He prefers to work within the possibilities of theatre rather than trying to make it something else. He has shunned the fashions of English theatre, avoiding both the Pinteresque concern with dramatizing mood and the Howard Brenton vision of theatre as a vehicle for politics. The English, he argues, can indulge in the rhetoric of propagandist drama because it's safe there: they're secure in a continuing culture which has hardly changed in hundreds of years.

'But here we're continually thrust into a situation of confrontation. Politics are so obtrusive here.'

He gestures out of the window. The British army barracks dominates Derry from the opposite bank of the Foyle. Below, the entrance to the Guildhall is protected by a perimeter of barbed wire.

'For people like ourselves, living close to such a fluid situation, definitions of identity have to be developed and analysed much more frequently.

'We've got to keep questioning until we find some kind of portmanteau term or until we find some kind of generosity that can embrace the whole island.

'That certainly is the ultimate aim, isn't it?'

In Interview with Paddy Agnew (1980)

Paddy Agnew: In the programme notes for *Translations* you cite a quotation from Martin Heidegger about the nature of language. This same quotation appears as the foreword to George Steiner's *After Babel*, a scholarly work about aspects of translation and language. How and why did you come to read Steiner?

Brian Friel: I came to *After Babel* because I was doing a translation of *Three Sisters* [Field Day, 1981]. Although I do not speak a word of Russian, I had been working on this play with the help of five standard English translations. It was a kind of act of love, but after a while I began to wonder exactly what I was doing. I think *Three Sisters* is a very important play, but I feel that the translations which we have received and inherited in some way have not much to do with the language which we speak in Ireland.

I think that the versions of *Three Sisters* which we see and read in this country always seem to be redolent of either Edwardian England or the Bloomsbury set. Somehow the rhythms of these versions do not match with the rhythms of our own speech patterns, and I think that they ought to, in some way. Even the most recent English translation again carries, of necessity, very strong English cadences and rhythms. This is something about which I feel strongly – in some way we are constantly overshadowed by the sound of English language, as well as by the printed word. Maybe this does not inhibit us, but it forms us and shapes us in a way that is neither healthy nor valuable for us.

The work I did on *Three Sisters* somehow overlapped into the working of the text of *Translations*.

PA: The fact that you opened *Translations* in Derry would imply that you felt the play had a relevance to the North, in general, and to Derry, in particular, which it does not have to the rest of Ireland, or to anywhere else for that matter?

BF: Not really, no. The reason that we wanted to rehearse in

Derry was because the town of Derry is close to the fictional location of the play. When the director, Art Ó Briain, came here he
felt this was the obvious place to rehearse this play. So we looked
around Derry and to our surprise the Guildhall were enthusiastic
about the venture.

PA: Do you feel then that the play has a relevance to places like
Belgium or Quebec, where there is a problem of two cultures?

BF: Yes, I think so. Those are two places where I would love to go
with this play. I am sure there are areas of Russia, perhaps Estonia
or Southern Russia, where their languages have faded, as has
Irish. Of course, a fundamental irony of this play is that it should
have been written in Irish.

PA: The old schoolmaster, Hugh, at one point says that 'certain
cultures expend on their vocabularies and syntax acquisitive energies and ostentations entirely lacking in their material lives'. Do
you feel that, in a sense, the loss of our Celtic background means
that we have lost a vital energy?

BF: What Hugh is saying there is that societies which do not have
material wealth or material stability are inclined to compensate
for this by the invention and use of a language which is more
ostentatious and opulent than the language of an economically
secure society. What I am talking about however is the relationship of this island to the neighbouring island. We have all been
educated in an English system; we are brought up in school reading Wordsworth, Shelley and Keats. These are formative influences on our lives and there is no possibility of escaping from this.

We must accept this. But we must make this primary recognition
and it is a recognition which we must never lose sight of: that there
is a foreignness in this literature; it is the literature of a different
race. If we assume that we have instant and complete access to that
literature, we are unfair to it and to ourselves. And we constantly
make that assumption because of the common language error.

If I can quote from the play, 'We must learn where we live. We
must make them [those new names] our own. We must make
them our new home.' That is, we must make these English language words distinctive and unique to us. My first concern is with
theatre and we certainly have not done this with theatre in Ireland. The only person who did so in this country was Synge.
Nobody since him has pursued this course with any persistence or

distinction, and indeed this is one of the problems of the theatre in this country. It is a new and young discipline for us and, apart from Synge, all our dramatists have pitched their voices for English acceptance and recognition.

This applied particularly to someone like Behan. However, I think that for the first time this is stopping, that there is some kind of confidence, some kind of coming together of Irish dramatists who are not concerned with this [ventriloquism], who have no interest in the English stage. We are talking to ourselves as we must and if we are overheard in America or England, so much the better.

PA: Does the same principle apply to other areas of Irish life, namely that we have not found our own voice?

BF: I suppose so, but probably the voice can only be found in letters, in the arts. Perhaps this is an artist's arrogance, but I feel that once the voice is found in literature, then it can move out and become part of the common currency.

PA: Is the English which we speak still 'full of the mythologies of fantasy and hope and self-deception'?

BF: I think so, certainly in our political lives.

PA: Is it wrong then to suggest that *Translations* is a political, polemical play?

BF: I really do not know. I am the last person to ask, really. Apparently *An Phoblacht* did a piece on it which says that the character of Doalty is the central figure, that a man who does not know the seven times table can still have a deep instinct which is true and accurate.

PA: Because he says, 'I've damned little to defend but he'll not put me out without a fight'?

BF: Something like that, I suppose. But someone else suggested to me that the key figure is Owen, who was described to me as a typical SDLP man, but people are entitled to take their own interpretation out of the play. Perhaps there is some kind of validity in that, that the figure of Owen is an SDLP man and that if he is then the task upon which he embarked was done with some kind of honour.

PA: In the end, in terms of the narrative, the colonial presence is malign. This would suggest that simply there will be no solution to the Irish problem until the British presence removes itself or is removed?

BF: We are not just talking about the present time and I am no expert in matters political, but in the long run of course I think that that is going to be true. There will be no solution until the British leave this island, but even when they have gone, the residue of their presence will still be with us. This is an area that we still have to resolve, and that brings us back to the question of language for this is one of the big inheritances which we have received from the British. In fact twenty miles from where we are sitting, you can hear very strong elements of Elizabethan English being spoken every day. The departure of the British army will have absolutely no bearing on the tongue that is spoken in that area. We must continually look at ourselves, recognize and identify ourselves. We must make English identifiably our own language.

PA: When Yolland describes his initial impressions of the Baile Beag community as being somewhere 'at its ease and with its own conviction and assurance', does that not imply some sort of nostalgia for Celtic Ireland?

BF: I have no nostalgia for that time. I think one should look back on the process of history with some kind of coolness. The only merit in looking back is to understand, how you are and where you are at this moment. Several people commented that the opening scenes of the play were a portrait of some sort of idyllic, Forest of Arden life. But this is a complete illusion, since you have on stage the representatives of a certain community – one is dumb, one is lame and one is alcoholic, a physical maiming which is a public representation of their spiritual deprivation.

PA: You talk of looking back on history with some sort of coolness. Is that what is implied by suggesting that 'it is not the literal past, the "facts" of history, that shape us, but images of the past embodied in language'?

BF: In some ways the inherited images of 1916, or 1690, control and rule our lives much more profoundly than the historical truth of what happened on those two occasions. The complication of that problem is how do we come to terms with it using an English language. For example, is our understanding of the Siege of Derry going to be determined by Macaulay's history of it, or is our understanding of Parnell going to be determined by [F. S. L.] Lyons's portrait of Parnell? This is a matter which will require a type of eternal linguistic vigilance.

PA: 'Confusion is not an ignoble condition,' says Hugh, but in the Irish context can we afford to be confused?

BF: I think most of us live in confusion. I live in confusion. Hugh's words are perhaps a fairly accurate description of how we all live, specifically at the present time. Other countries perhaps have access to more certainties than we have at the moment. I was talking specifically about Ireland.

Programme Note for Tom Murphy's
The Blue Macushla (1980)

'We will stick to our own and the soot, as we did through the centuries. We have a love of our own, and we will keep it! Lord! Lord! Deserters!'

A Crucial Week in The Life of a Grocer's Assistant (1969)

'For I have dreamed of one who'll come through these woods and find me . . . A man with eyes flaming green . . . Burning equally for righteousness and love for me . . . His shining purest youth being acknowledged even by the grass that loves his tread . . . So slender, so certain, so perfect.'

The Morning After Optimism (1971)

The most distinctive, the most restless, the most obsessive imagination at work in the Irish theatre today is Tom Murphy's. It is essentially a Gaelic imagination – antic, bleak, agitated, bewildered, capable of great cruelty and great compassion. It is the kind of imagination that in a different culture would probably find its voice in music or painting. In Ireland it inclines intuitively to the service of theatre – or religion. Both seem to offer it passing release, public consolation, and the illusion of completion.

Tom Murphy's first play, *On the Outside,* written in collaboration with a friend, appeared twenty-one years ago, when Murphy was twenty-four. (Ever since he has used his titles as early-warning signals of coming anguish: *A Whistle in The Dark*, *The Orphans*, *Famine*, *A Crucial Week*, *The Morning after Optimism.*) *On the Outside* has been his claimed territory and vantage point ever since – more an achieved state of mind than a physical location – and from there he has explored the fate of Fallen Man, Eden's expatriates, pining for restoration, hung between the 'soot' and the 'perfection'.

It is a play about two young men, Frank and Joe, whose girl-friends are inside the dance-hall, a [William] Trevor-type Ball-room of Romance. But the young men cannot join their girls because they haven't the price of admission. So they spend the night outside the hall, in limbo, listening to the distant siren music, sustaining themselves with bitter jokes, until the dance is over. Then Joe in the last line of the play says, 'Come on out of here to hell.' Any certainty seems preferable.

Fifteen years and five plays later Murphy wrote a companion piece, *On the Inside,* set this time inside the dance-hall. But despite the gained admission nothing has changed in the interven-ing years. The play opens with the line, 'Did you see anyone you like?' and closes with 'What is this thing called love?' One lives on the outside and pines for the inside. But once that inside is achieved it in turn becomes an outside. The only constant in life is the yearning for something that must be better than what is. The only certainty is that that yearning can never be satisfied.

What distinguishes Murphy from everybody else writing for the theatre in this country today – or indeed from any other contem-porary playwright that I know of – is his theatrical language and the pure theatricality of that language. It is as close as one can get, or should wish to get, to poetry in drama. It has the resonance and tautness of true poetry but it remains faithful to the primary responsibilities of its setting and function. The problem he sets himself, particularly in plays like *Optimism* and *The Sanctuary Lamp,* is enormous: to make articulate and theatrically valid char-acters whose lives are obsessed with Innocence and Forgiveness and Guilt and Perfectibility. And he solves it by the creation of a factitious speech, almost a private dialect, that is both capable of conveying these enormous and hazardous burdens and is at the same time perfectly accessible to an audience. Indeed, so artfully does he accomplish this that the listener is unaware of its artifi-ciality and uniqueness. Language and character are a unity. Each is a creation of the other. That is an achievement that Synge would have been proud of.

In his Preface to *Four Plays* Dürrenmatt writes: 'People call nihilistic what is merely uncomfortable . . . Today's author, however, can no longer confine himself with good conscience to whispering pleasant stories and praising the beautiful landscape. Unfortunately, too, he cannot get out of this mad race in order to sit by the wayside, writing the pure poetry demanded of him by all the non-poets. Fear, worry, and above all anger open his mouth wide.' Again and again Murphy's work grapples with those fears and worries and angers that all of us share. And every time he opens his mouth we do well to listen.

In Interview with Victoria Radin (1981)

Brian Friel qualifies his every statement. He thinks that maybe it's because he's Irish. He has a theory – and he's by no means the first or last to hold it – that the Irish feel uneasy in the English language. It hasn't for them the same reverberations, associations, accretions, of centuries.

In fact, English has been Ireland's tongue for only a couple of hundred years. Joyce was uneasy in it, too. Stephen Dedalus feels he comes off second-best in his dialogue with the English Dean of Studies in *A Portrait of the Artist as a Young Man* (1916): 'The language in which we are speaking is his before it is mine . . . His language, so familiar and so foreign, will always be for me an acquired speech. I have not made or accepted its words. My voice holds them at bay. My soul frets in the shadow of his language.' The Irish must mint English afresh, and that can be an advantage for their writers. Though Brian Friel doesn't say so, Ireland has given the world rather more than its fair share of good writers.

He is one of them – probably the best living Irish dramatist (bar Beckett) and among the best in the British Isles. But like most good – and some not so good – Irish writers, he's not well known in Britain, much better in the US. It was in the sleek pages of *The New Yorker* that he published through the 1960s the short stories of Irish country life, rather Chekhovian, that enabled him to give up schoolteaching. And it was on Broadway, and on tour throughout the US for some time afterwards, that his fourth play, *Philadelphia, Here I Come!*, was the hit of 1965–66.

That was a long time ago, he says; he doesn't like talking about it. In that play Friel, who likes technical experiments, used the device of the *alter ego* that Peter Nichols has lately picked up again in *Passion Play* of having an inner and outer self played by two actors. Later, in London, *Philadelphia* fizzled out. 'It generates a disproportionate amount of emotion and charm,' said this newspaper. Which must be the ultimate in critical stinginess.[1]

In a way, says Friel, it would be better if the Irish were considered by the English to be truly foreign – which they are and which he's happy to be – instead of resident clowns. But no, he doesn't exactly think there's a *prejudice* against the Irish here. Just a preconception or idea of what an Irish play or its writer should be like. A sort of Brendan Behan, a joker, of whom Ken Tynan could write – Friel seems to remember it very well – 'he scatters words the way a drunken sailor scatters money'.[2] Congreve, Farquhar, Sheridan, Wilde and Shaw – they all strutted and danced. The Irish don't speak to each other, they pitch their voices to be heard outside their island. When Friel listens to Hugh Leonard, he hears Neil Simon.

Friel is much more in the tradition of Joyce, Yeats and one of his cronies, the poet Seamus Heaney, by believing in the magical properties of language, the Word. He believes that it touches latent sensibilities and stirs them into a new kind of life. It's as if – though he'd never be guilty of such a round or unqualified statement – Ireland could be *saved* by language. In fifty years there will be more accretions, in two hundred – if English is still spoken – many more.

He's from the North – from Londonderry. Twelve years ago, fortuitously, just before the Troubles began, he moved with his wife Anne and five children to a village, three miles away, across the border. He's confused about the writer's role in the Troubles.

If we must talk about it, he thinks the English will pull out of Northern Ireland eventually, but there ought to be a time-scale imposed. He was on the civil rights march that became Bloody Sunday and felt that the British army hadn't *quite* exercised due restraint.

The Freedom of the City – one of his three overtly political plays – was about that. Writing them was like some kind of emotional inflammation, the way you get a sore throat as protection against a more serious infection. Was it, he wondered, an abdication of real, more humane things, under the pressure and hysteria of the moment? What did I think?

He is apt to ask you questions like that – and not just rhetorically. He is a medium-sized man with a slight Northern lilt and a very direct blue gaze. Sometimes it feels inquisitorial – he never, says one of his writer friends, the poet and professor of English, Seamus Deane, stops gathering information. It seems to be partly genuine interest and partly writer's antennae. At times during our interview I wondered who would finally get written up.

He was in town to watch the rehearsals of *Faith Healer*, which opens at the Royal Court tomorrow, and to help at the casting of *Translations* which previews at the Hampstead Theatre Club at the end of April. A Friel mini-festival, which I predict will anchor him in this country, but one never knows.

Despite the presence of James Mason in the title role (in his first stage appearance in thirty years, by all accounts excellent), *Faith Healer* flopped on Broadway: Walter Kerr, praising it,[3] said that it required work from the audience, which can't have helped. It is a technically risky play, consisting of four monologues spoken in turn by three characters – the faith healer, his wife and his manager, who are played at the Court by Patrick Magee, Helen Mirren and Stephen Lewis.

It's the faith healer who has the final word. By then it's clear that he's lying – or lying about facts. The moral truth, however unpalatable, is his: just as it's often the province of any other shaman, shrink, quack, con man or artist. Friel for once doesn't fudge the fact that the faith healer could be a metaphor for the writer and his writing: his sense that he is a medium, perhaps a victim, of something outside himself, his selfishness towards the people who are close to him – or, why funk the issue, love him? That was why he wrote it.

Friel was reading through the ordnance survey of Ireland when Stephen Rea asked if he had any new plays about. Rea, born in Belfast, has been a friend ever since he acted in *The Freedom of the City* at the Court [1973] and Friel's *Aristocrats* at the Abbey [1979]. The Belfast Arts Council had offered him some money to set up a touring company in Northern Ireland. Out of that grew Field Day, jointly administered by Friel and Rea, and their first production, *Translations*, which was the hit of the Irish theatre and of the Dublin Festival last year.

It is set in Ballybeg in the 1830s, a Gaelic Ireland, just at the point that the English were colonizing it [further] by setting up English-language schools, and translating place names. And the bitter irony is, of course, that the play is written in English. Friel speaks Gaelic, but is not soft in the head. The purpose of Field Day, he says, after tiptoeing round it – he has the sense that he should have very clear objectives written like samplers above the bed – is to provide a brave and vibrant theatre that in some way expresses his country. He thinks of Yeats and the Moscow Art Theatre.

For their next production – they're beginning to call it Friels on Wheels – he is translating *Three Sisters* into Irish English. Chekhov in English is so Bloomsbury. It could even be that the Irish are closer to the Russian playwright. A different kind of Chekhov could emerge. 'Maybe not,' says Friel. 'But I feel perhaps yes.'

In Interview with Elgy Gillespie (1981)

Behind the iron fence the Guildhall looks immaculate and hollow, like a film set façade. The laughing security staff unlock gate and door, urging you down a stately hall and up sweeping marble steps. Stained-glass windows depicting captains and kings, in a manner tactlessly overt, proclaim debts to bodies across the water.

The new play being rehearsed and performed there is Brian Friel's own translation of Chekhov's *Three Sisters* and it is to make music to Irish ears as the second Irish production of the Field Day Theatre Company, which has scored so ubiquitously with *Translations*. That play starred Stephen Rea as Owen, but this time Friel's co-director in Field Day is himself directing. So both Field Day directors have, to an extent, submerged original selfhood and personal development for the good of the company production, which opens here next Tuesday and comes to Dublin for the Theatre Festival.

Brian Friel slipped out to the corridor and boiled the kettle for tea. In his fifties now, his high-cheeked face seems to acquire more Thady Quill puckishness as time goes on. He has an exceedingly gentle manner, and a beautiful voice with very musical modulations. When he split his evening pants at the Harvey Awards last spring, he described himself as 'backing out of the limelight', and does not give any credence to success. ('For the writer there is no such thing as success just as there is no "success" in the rain falling or the sun shining.')

Until Field Day was launched, Friel loathed press interviews and never gave them if he could help it. It's easy to see why: he is so mild and equivocal in manner that it is easy, even inevitable, for journalists to put their own bias or construction upon his words by quite unconsciously giving them certain inflections. He is the opposite of 'cityish' witty, urbane, forceful. But he is not doctrinairely political in a republican sense, as you might have

96

decided upon the reported evidence, and in any case he has himself admitted that he always comes to regret the causes he involves himself in.

His passionate involvement in Field Day, we can safely hazard, is not about nationalism in a narrow way. It's about questioning everything, just the way he questions everything as he talks. The journalists would easily put these questions down as statements, if they were taping them and relaying word for word. This, he explains, is why he's no good at them [interviews]. 'Things seem so much more definite in the way I'm quoted in interviews.'

So why, to ask the obvious question, had they chosen *Three Sisters*, and what was so wrong with other translations? 'We wanted a classic, we felt a classic would be what Field Day needed at this point. We're still defining ourselves by exploration and we both still feel this development is an integral part of our career.' But so much energy to be expended in the drag of touring, the recounting of box office receipts (at which neither Rea nor Friel excels), when they could be acting, writing?

Friel makes a little movement of his head, approximating to a shrug, the better to downplay commitment. 'Oh, it's very draining. But I suppose we must be getting something back from it . . .' If he were forced to be more definite about Field Day's artistic and political aims? He wasn't sure what those two things mean, or how they move in relation to each other, he quietly replied.

Elgy Gillespie: Oh, so you just don't want to be preachy about it?
Brian Friel: I'd love to be preachy but I'm not sure what the sermon is. We can only define afterwards what the sermon is.

After the tour will come *Angel* for Stephen Rea, a film with a script by Neil Jordan, in which he plays a saxophonist besotted with Charlie 'Bird' Parker. But for Friel? 'Afterwards I'll have to get my own life back into shape, I suppose.'

Field Day emerged quite naturally, when the Arts Council suggested Stephen Rea as the man to come over and play in *Translations*. The Guildhall turned out to be the ideal place to rehearse, generous as it is with facilities and goodwill towards them. Rea didn't want to just come, and go back to London again.

BF: Both of us felt there was some tiny little space we might fill that we could focus the whole North thing on . . . but we knew we must have impermanence built in. This could be our last play, or we could go on for another twenty years. In fact, Tom Mullarkey's plans for a new Derry theatre are still knocking about the Guildhall somewhere, awaiting the finance to help found a home for a second Northern rep company – but that wouldn't be relevant to Field Day.

We don't think it's necessarily of value to have a building to offer up piety towards; no matter how modest, you'd have to continually ask yourself what to do with it, you couldn't just do something or do nothing. It's part of the fluxiness to not know if we'll be doing something or not, and we feel fluxiness is the most important thing for us now.

EG: So there might easily not be a Field Day by next year?

BF: If a great new play emerged tomorrow, especially if it was a Northern play, we'd jump at it. Or else we might put out a magazine or do something completely different.

Nevertheless, Friel and Rea were exhausted and depleted at the end of their last tour, and also had very serious money problems. They have now acquired a business manager, Noel McKenna, to take care of that end, and they rejoice in grants from both Northern and Southern Arts Councils as well as help from Derry's city fathers. They find nothing sullying about the promotional end. They have also expanded Field Day's board to include poets Seamus Heaney, Seamus Deane and Tom Paulin, and the BBC producer Davy Hammond. Friel says he is quite unmoved both by the spectacular acclaim for *Translations* at the National Theatre, and by the euphoria that greeted its first night last year in Derry.

BF: I'm too old for euphoria, and the spectacle of first nights in particular. They belong to Broadway. Euphoria on first nights makes me wonder what's wrong with the play.

EG: Of course *Translations* was an easy, accessible, lovable sort of play?

BF: It's deliberately very traditional, with three acts and a rural setting. I think that, as Stephen and I have put it before, we are talking to ourselves really, and if America and England overhear us, that's us delighted.

Translations swung instantly into warmth and heat, as Friel puts it; talking to himself – 'but not in a narrow Sinn Féin way' – he was surprised at the breadth of its reception. Whereas the more austere, less playlike *Faith Healer* had a more hazardous, tumultuous career and a bad reception. You feel, Friel says, as you do about a sickly child, for a panned play.

BF: But as [Tyrone] Guthrie said, a playwright only survives as a body of work. Now the thing is this one. Your children grow up and leave home after their run; the newborn babe-in-arms is the one you concentrate all your love upon.

EG: What about your lifelong love affair with Chekhov, so evident in the echoes of *Aristocrats*? Why must he be rewritten for us?

BF: It *is* a work of love. The first purpose in doing *Three Sisters* like this is because for a group of Irish actors, only American or English texts are available. If it's an English text of a Russian scenario, there's a double assumption there. I felt we should be able to short-circuit this double assumption so that they [the actors] can assume a language that can simply flow out of them.

Of course [Elisabeth] Fen is perfect for England, but if you do use that one you must get your actors to assume English accents because it's English music. As English as Elgar. The officers say, 'Jolly good. Wasn't it splendid?'

EG: Isn't that explanation going to sound, perhaps, exaggerated and caused simply by nationalistic sentiment?

BF: Yes, I'll have to be careful of that. It's a risk. But there's the other thing, that the received method of playing Chekhov is just to take up a stance on the down-stage right or left, stare into the middle distance and talk desultorily about philosophical questions. Whereas there should be a great reality, about the acting as well as about the words. Again, there's a calculated risk about tackling it a new way.

It's all a question of music. The audience will hear a different music to anything they've heard in Chekhov before.

EG: Have you resorted to a literal translation of the actual Russian text?

BF: No, I sat down at my desk with six English versions in front of me. But on one occasion, in particular, I did: when I wasn't sure what to do about the soldier bringing in a samovar as a gift to the sisters. Samovars are normally given only to long-married matrons. So why should everyone be shocked if you don't happen to know samovars aren't given to girls? I wanted to be both absolutely faithful, and true to naturalism.

In the end I just funked it. I put: 'Would you look at what he's got her! A samovar! Oh my God! That's what you give to old maids!', which made it different again. The ideal condition would be to have a playwright who was fluent in Russian. But if you have to forgo the one, I think it's better for the translator to be a dramatist. There are bigger truths beyond that of the literal translation.

In Interview with Ray Comiskey (1982)

The visitor to Derry's Guildhall has to pass under the disapproving gaze of Queen Victoria. [. . .] Next week the Guildhall will be host to a new play by a man from a rather different cultural lineage. Brian Friel's latest work, a farce called *The Communication Cord*, which deals with the problem of language and communication, will receive its world première there. But if Friel's background is quite different from what the Guildhall stands for, his play is part of his own efforts and those of the theatre company he founded with Stephen Rea, Field Day, to focus attention on aspects of the various traditions here today and likely to be changed, but not gone, tomorrow.

In its underlying linguistic concerns the new work has some common ground with the playwright's earlier *Translations*, and it fits in with the emerging interests of Field Day.

Ray Comiskey: So how did the company come about?
Brian Friel: It hadn't any formal beginnings, in that Stephen and I sat down and said, 'Now what we must do for the next three or five years is this, and we must attempt it in this kind of way.' It began more casually, where a group of people with a kind of intuitive understanding of various things found themselves coming together on the enterprise.
RC: Could you explain that?
BF: We think of ourselves as Derry-based, northern-focused, but absolutely in terms of the whole island. The Derry base is important because in some way Derry is an important psychic town on this island. The northern focus is very important because – and what I'm doing now is articulating things that we didn't begin with, but which emerged with the practice – both Stephen and I feel, maybe in some kind of silly way, that the North is going to be one of the determining features of the future of this island.

In practical terms, it means rehearsing and opening in Derry, having round the enterprise a predominance of northern people, and touring from Coleraine to Kerry, but always with the one constant, which is the theatre.

RC: Would the North's likely influence on the future be due to the old moulds being questioned more there than in the South?

BF: Yes, I think they are. Field Day is not about changing the North – I hate using grandiose terms like this – but in some way the very fact that it's located in the North and has its reservations about it, and that it works in the South and has its reservations about it, it's like, as somebody said, an artistic fifth province.

We're not talking in precise political terms at all. We're talking about some kind of awareness, some kind of sense of the country, what is this island about, north and south, and what are our attitudes to it. Leaving aside the Chekhov, the first play we did, *Translations*, was about how this country found a certain shape.

This farce is another look at the shape this country is in now. There's a strong element of satire in it, so we're talking about, not political realities, but perhaps, insofar as any theatre can affect anything, some kind of minute little adjusting attitudes.

RC: About cultural realities as they affect a personal sense of identity?

BF: Yes. But there is the difficulty of avoiding pretentious language when dealing with a subject like this. You find yourself saying extreme things that you need to qualify immediately.

RC: It has been said that you are sick of the term 'national identity', and what the hell does it mean?

BF: It means something very important, because it's your national ID in some way, isn't it?

RC: How does this farce, your first venture into the form for which, you have said, you had no models, fit into this picture?

BF: Well, a farce is a very serious enterprise. It's supposed to entertain and be very funny, and if it isn't it has failed as a farce . . . (*Laughs*) You say that and get it out of the way. But then, I think that it's a perfectly valid way of looking at people in Ireland today, that our situation has become so absurd and so . . . crass that it seems to me it might be a valid way to talk and write about it.

RC: What are the attractions of satire in this?

BF: There's always a strong satirical element in farce. It's not sub-tle, like you get in comedy. It's very broad, and in farce it's simply the satire that says, 'Man is an unthinking animal, he has no intel-ligence and he acts intuitively and instinctively, and he doesn't know why he does it; so if something happens he just responds to it in the same way.'

RC: With this it goes back to the question of communication in *The Communication Cord*?

BF: It does. It's an extension of that. In other words, what func-tion does language have then? In the case of *Translations* we were talking about the function of a fractured language, an acquired language and a lost language. In this case it's saying – I don't want to go back to the grandiose language – but it's saying, again, that perhaps communication isn't possible at all.

RC: Communication in the sense in which it's spoken about in this play?

BF: Right. One of the lines in the play is 'Maybe silence is the per-fect discourse.' (*Shrugs*) Maybe.

RC: The very act of creating the play is, in itself, a denial of that line.

Behind the hall in which the farce will be performed, in a big, echoing room overlooking the Foyle, the cast of eight were rehearsing under the eye of the director, Joe Dowling. It's an often tedious business, doing things over and over, getting lines, inter-pretation, positions, actions and – particularly in farce – the tim-ing right to make it work. [. . .]

This is the final week of rehearsals, known as the technical. The cast will have moved into the great hall to work on the actual stage, getting accustomed to the set and props, the doors and stairs of the restored traditional cottage in which the action takes place; and at the week's end the lighting has to be worked in. [. . .]

Then comes the première next Tuesday, after which it moves to Belfast's Opera House on 27 September, followed by a tour of the north and south, finally reaching Dublin at the Gaiety on 1 November and winding up with a week at the Everyman in Cork. But the fact that it will not be a part of the Dublin Theatre Festi-val has led to all sorts of rumours down here, so the question was put to Brian Friel to answer himself.

BF: There's absolutely nothing sinister about it. We were invited to the Festival and we considered at one stage that we might go. We would have liked to go because we got a very generous offer from the Dublin Theatre Festival which would have solved all the financial problems for us this year, but it was simpler for us to stick to the tour we had outlined. That's really all there was to it. We will go to Dublin when the time comes.

RC: Finance, then, remains a perennial problem for Field Day?

BF: About two-thirds comes from the Arts Council in Belfast, with the bulk of the remainder coming from its counterpart in Dublin, not to mention some modest amounts from the Northern Ireland Tourist Board, Irish Shell and subscriptions from programme advertisers. It hangs over plans now being explored to tour America, and it means a hand-to-mouth existence for the company.

Arts councils of their nature never give you all the money you need, and that's fair enough. There's always a gap between what they give and what you require. Of course, I worry endlessly about it, but in the long term I don't really worry all that much, because I think we'll survive as long as we need to survive.

RC: As long as the will is there?

BF: Right. If we were getting a million dollars tonight it would be great for this year. But we're not looking to an endless future. That's what I'm really saying.

In Interview with Fintan O'Toole (1982)

Brian Friel lives in Muff, County Donegal, a few miles across the border from Derry. The house, which he had built in the mid-1960s, is clearly a product of the success in America of *Philadelphia, Here I Come!*, the play which first brought him international recognition. Its design mirrors the best of that decade. It is bright, angular, with open spaces and polished wood. The sitting room, where the interview took place, is situated at the side of the house overlooking the River Foyle, a room built to make the most of the meagre Donegal sunshine. The Friel family will shortly move to an older and smaller house twenty miles further into County Donegal.

Brian Friel was born in Omagh, County Tyrone, in 1929. When he was ten years old, his father, a schoolteacher, took up a new job in Derry and the family moved to a house in the Bogside. His mother's family, however, came from Donegal, a place he has always felt a strong affinity with. He attended teacher training college in Belfast, and taught until 1960, when he left to become a full-time writer. In 1982 he was appointed to the Arts Council by the Taoiseach, Charles Haughey.

Field Day Theatre Company was formed by Friel and actor Stephen Rea in 1980, and so far all of its productions – *Translations*, *Three Sisters* (a translation from Chekhov), and *The Communication Cord* – have been of Friel's work. Its directors (Seamus Deane, Tom Paulin, Seamus Heaney, David Hammond, Brian Friel and Stephen Rea) are all from Northern Ireland.[1] Field Day's tour next year, however, will be of a new play by another Northern writer.

Fintan O'Toole: The first thing I wanted to ask you was about the sense of place in your work and the fact that so many of your characters seem to lack a sense of place, to be dislocated. Does that have any parallel in your own life?

Brian Friel: That's a real academic's question, isn't it? I'll try to answer it. Seamus Deane has written a number of essays on me, and that's one of his persistent points, that I'm some sort of displaced person, you know? If there are parallels in my own life I don't know. There is certainly a sense of rootlessness and impermanence. It may well be the inheritance of being a member of the Northern minority. That could be one of the reasons, where you are certainly at home but in some sense exile is imposed on you. That may be a reason, I mean I'm groping at answers to this. In some kind of a way I think Field Day has grown out of that sense of impermanence, of people who feel themselves native to a province or certainly to an island but in some way feel that a disinheritance is offered to them.

FO'T: Is Field Day then an attempt to reclaim that inheritance?

BF: Yeah, but the difficulty is what to reclaim. You can't deposit fealty to a situation like the Northern situation that you don't believe in. Then you look south of the border and that enterprise is in so many ways distasteful. And yet both places are your home, so you are an exile in your home in some kind of sense. It may be an inheritance from a political situation. I think it may very well be and I think the people that are gathered around Field Day – there are six of them – I don't want to speak for the other five, but I think this could be a common sense to all of them. Someone has suggested, maybe it was [Tom] Paulin, that it's a kind of an attempt to create a fifth province to which artistic and cultural loyalty can be offered.

FO'T: There's also a close sense of family in your plays and of the kind of bonds that the family imposes on the individual.

BF: Maybe it's part of the same thing again, that there's some kind of instinctive sense of home being central to the life and yet at the same time home being a place of great stress and great alienation. I'm not really very good at this kind of question, Fintan, because the question's a kind of abstract based on a body of work, isn't it, and I sort of look from enterprise to enterprise, from job to job, you know what I mean? So it's really a kind of an academic's question, isn't it?

FO'T: So, do you never look back on your work and attempt to pick things out?

BF: No, not at all. Only when you find, for example, that categories are being imposed on you, for example after three plays in particular – after *Faith Healer*, which was kind of an austere enterprise, *Translations*, which was offered pieties that I didn't intend for it, and then *Three Sisters* – in some way I felt I'm being corralled into something here. By other people. And this was one of the reasons I wanted to attempt a farce.

FO'T: Were you consciously attempting an antidote to *Translations* when you were writing *The Communication Cord*?

BF: Oh yes. Well, consciously at two levels. Firstly for Field Day, because I felt it would be appropriate for Field Day to have something like that at this point but also from my own point of view, because I was being categorized in some sort of a way that I didn't feel easy about, and it seemed to me that a farce would disrupt that kind of categorizing. There's risks involved in doing that sort of thing. I think it's a risky enterprise doing a farce. But I think it's worth it.

FO'T: When you started off with *The Communication Cord*, were you aware of trying to use the mechanisms of classical farce?

BF: Yes, it's something like a Meccano set – you get on with various pieces of it and you put them all together. Maybe it's different from the usual farce in that the play itself was to some extent an attempt to illustrate a linguistic thesis. But apart from that it's just a regular farce, isn't it?

FO'T: Yes, but it does also carry on a concern with language that has been evident in your work for the past five or six years. So it's a farce that is also, in one sense, to be taken very seriously.

BF: It's a form to which very little respect is offered and it was important to do it for that reason, not to make it respectable, but to release me into what I bloody well wanted, to attempt it, to have a go at it.

FO'T: Were you aware of almost being canonized after *Translations*?

BF: Ach, not at all, ah no, that's very strong. But it was treated much too respectfully. You know, when you get notices especially from outside the island, saying, 'If you want to know what happened in Cuba, if you want to know what happened in Chile, if you want to know what happened in Vietnam, read *Translations*', that's nonsense. And I just can't accept that sort of pious rubbish.

FO'T: I was wondering whether your concern with language, indeed with your profession as a playwright, stemmed from a re-

examination of that profession. You said in 1972 that you were
thinking of going back to writing short stories instead of plays.

BF: Ah, I don't know. The whole language one is a very tricky
one. The whole issue of language is a very problematic one for us
all on this island. I had grandparents who were native Irish speak-
ers and also two of the four grandparents were illiterate. It's very
close, you know, I actually remember two of them. And to be so
close to illiteracy and to a different language is a curious experience. And in some way I don't think we've resolved it. We haven't
resolved it on this island for ourselves. We flirt with the English
language, but we haven't absorbed it and we haven't regurgitated
it in some kind of way. It's accepted outside the island, you see, as
'our great facility with the English language' – Tynan said we used
it like drunken sailors, you know that kind of image – that's all
old rubbish.² A language is much more profound than that. It's
not something we produce for the entertainment of outsiders. And
that's how Irish theatre is viewed, indeed, isn't it?

FO'T: It is very often. And isn't it the dilemma of the modern Irish
playwright that to actually make a decent living out of writing
plays you have to find an audience in Britain and the States, while
the enterprise that you're involved in is more about trying to write
primarily for an Irish audience?

BF: Are you confusing an economic dilemma with an artistic
dilemma? Is that what you're saying?

FO'T: Well, doesn't the fact of having to make a living force certain conditions on you?

BF: It doesn't, no. Not in the slightest. Because in the case of
Translations I was really sure that this was the first enterprise that
Field Day was going to do and I was sure we were in deep trouble
with that play. We thought, Field Day will never even get a lift-off
because of this play, because here is a play set in 1833, set in a
hedge-school – you have to explain the terminology to people outside the island, indeed to people inside the island too, so I thought
we were on a real financial loss here. But that is part of the enterprise, and this is one of the reasons why I attempted the translation of Chekhov. It's back to the political problem – it's our
proximity to England, it's how we have been pigmented in our
theatre with the English experience, with the English language, the
use of the English language, the understanding of words: the

whole cultural burden that every word in the English language carries is slightly different to our burden. Joyce talks in the *Portrait* of his resentment of the [English] Jesuit priest because '[h]is language, so familiar and so foreign, will always be for me an acquired speech', and so on.

FO'T: Did theatre come before short stories?

BF: No, I wrote stories first. I know now why I stopped writing short stories. It was at the point when I recognized how difficult they were. It would have meant a whole reappraisal. I mean, I was very much under the influence, as everyone at the time was, of [Sean] O'Faolain and [Frank] O'Connor, particularly. O'Connor dominated our lives. I suppose they [Friel's short stories] really were some kind of imitation of O'Connor's work. I'm just guessing at it, but I think at some point round about that period, the recognition of the difficulty of the thing, you know, that maybe there was the need for the discovery of a voice and that I was just echoing somebody else.

FO'T: What was the effect for you of suddenly, with your fourth play, having a great success and productions in America and becoming, at least for a time, a famous playwright?

BF: We'd need to be very careful about language. It [*Philadelphia, Here I Come!*] was a very successful play, and it's a play that in some kind of way haunts you too – people say, 'Oh yes, you're the man that wrote the play called *Philadelphia Story*, aren't you?' – so, famous and successful, I don't know.[3]

FO'T: Did you see it again when it was revived in the Abbey recently?

BF: I did, yeah.

FO'T: What was it like, seeing it again?

BF: I've really no interest in it at all. None whatsoever. I would go to a thing like that out of duty to the actors and to the theatre, but I've really no interest in the enterprise itself. I would feel minor irritations at the way things are written or expressed but no interest at all. Even things like *The Communication Cord*, which are still running, I have no interest in it really. It's finished and it is as it is, and I'm drawn on to the next enterprise.

FO'T: You wrote in the 1960s I suppose four plays which concentrated on different aspects of love – *Philadelphia*, *The Loves of Cass McGuire*, *Lovers* and *Crystal and Fox*. You then stopped writing about love [see above, p. 47]. Was it just that you had said all you wanted to say?

BF: I just don't know the answer to that. I don't think there's a point when you say, 'I've nothing more to say about that', because I don't think you start from that premise and say I've got this to say about anything. You don't have anything to say about anything. You delve into a particular corner of yourself that's dark and uneasy, and you articulate the confusions and the unease of that particular period. When you do that, that's finished and you acquire other corners of unease and discontent. There are continuing obsessions, like the political thing is a continuing obsession, and I've written two or three demonstrably political plays. And I keep saying to myself I'm never going to write another political play because it's too transient and because I'm confused about it myself, but I know damn well and I'm sure I'll have another shot at it again sometime.

FO'T: With *The Freedom of the City*, which was obviously a very complex play, are you afraid that in certain circumstances an audience might take a very crude and a very blunt political message from it?

BF: That wouldn't worry me anyway. 'Did that play of mine send out / Certain men [the English shot]?' – that sort of thing wouldn't worry me at all.[4] I think one of the problems with that play was that the experience of Bloody Sunday wasn't adequately distilled in me. I wrote it out of some kind of heat and some kind of immediate passion that I would want to have quieted a bit before I did it. It was really – do you remember that time? – it was a very emotive time. It was really a shattering experience that the British army, this disciplined instrument, would go in as they did that time and shoot thirteen people. To be there on that occasion and – I didn't actually see people get shot – but I mean, to have to throw yourself on the ground because people are firing at you is a very terrifying experience. Then the whole cover-up afterwards was shattering too. We still have some kind of belief that the law is above reproach. We still believe that the academy is above reproach in some way, don't we?

FO'T: Your active involvement in politics was in the 1960s in the Nationalist Party?

BF: Yeah, I was a member of the Nationalist Party for several years. I don't remember how long. Those were very dreary days because the Nationalist Party . . . it's hard to describe what it was. I suppose it held on to some kind of little faith, you know. It wasn't even sure what the faith was, and it was a very despised enterprise by everybody. We used to meet once a month wherever it was in a grotty wee room and there'd be four or five old men who'd sit there and mull over things. It was really hopeless.

FO'T: Did you ever regret the fact that you moved to Donegal from Derry shortly before the troubles began?

BF: I regretted it in many ways, yes. I think it was in '68, and the trouble began in '69 and we might have been better to be in there. Just to be part of the experience. Instead of driving into a civil rights march, coming out your front door and joining it might have been more real. It would have been less deliberate and less conscious than doing it from here.

FO'T: Coming back to what I was asking you earlier about your recent plays, which seem largely concerned with your own craft, *Faith Healer* was first staged in 1979 in New York. Was that a reflection of a concern with the power of the writer, with what you yourself do?

BF: I suppose it has to be. It was some kind of a metaphor for the art, the craft of writing, or whatever it is. And the great confusion we all have about it, those of us who are involved in it. How honourable and how dishonourable it can be. And it's also a pursuit that, of necessity, has to be very introspective, and as a consequence it leads to great selfishness. So that you're constantly, as I'm doing at this moment, saying something and listening to yourself saying it, and the third eye is constantly watching you. And it's a very dangerous thing because in some way it perverts whatever natural freedom you might have, and that natural freedom must find its expression in the written word. So there's an exploration of that – I mean the element of the charlatan that there is in all creative work.

FO'T: And even more so in the theatre because even at a distance you're acting as a showman?

BF: Yes. It's a very vulgar medium, in the Latin sense, and it's also vulgar, I think, too, in the accepted sense. But I think it also has satisfactions that you wouldn't find as a novelist or as a poet. It's a very attractive enterprise to be involved in. You would find that even as a critic, because they're very attractive people. It's a very essential kind of life because it's giving everything to this one enterprise and once it's over then we go on to something else. It's essentially human in some way.

FO'T: Of the six members of the Field Day Board only yourself and Stephen Rea are actively involved in theatre.

BF: That's right. I think the important defining thing about them all is that they're all Northern people.

FO'T: What is it about the South of Ireland that makes it impossible for you to give your loyalty to it?

BF: Well, of course I have loyalty to it, because in some way it's the old parent who is now beginning to ramble. In some way it could be adjusted and I think it could be made very exciting, I think. But I think it requires the Northern thing to complete it. I'm talking about the whole Northern thing.

FO'T: You're saying then that there are certain qualities that are peculiar to Northerners and not found in the South?

BF: Yes. I think the qualities are – I don't believe for one minute in Northern hard-headedness or any of that nonsense – but I think that if you have a sense of exile, that brings with it some kind of alertness and some kind of eagerness and some kind of hunger. And if you are in possession you can become, maybe, placid about some things. And I think those are the kind of qualities that, maybe, Field Day can express. Does this make any sense to you?

FO'T: Yes, it does. Do you think that that sense of exile gives you access as an artist to a more fundamental and widespread sense of alienation?

BF: Yeah, but the contradiction in that is that we are trying to make a home. So that we aspire to a home condition in some way. We don't think that exile is practical. We think that exile is miserable in fact. And what's constantly being offered to us, particularly in the North, and this is one of the problems for us, is that we are constantly being offered the English home; we have been educated by the English home and we have been pigmented by an English home. To a much greater extent than you have been. And the rejection of all that, and the rejection into what, is the big problem.

FO'T: What is home for you? Is it a sense of a group of people with a common purpose? Is that in itself going to give you some sense of belonging?

BF: I think now at this point it would, but once I would achieve it and once it would be acquired then I'd be off again.

FO'T: There is in a way a contradiction for you, isn't there, because it seems necessary for you as a writer to have a sense of being on the outside, and yet you're striving with Field Day to transcend that?

BF: I think there is some kind of, there is the possibility of a cultural whole available to us – w-h-o-l-e, we're living in the other one [hole]. How to achieve that and how to contribute to that is one of the big problems, and the problem is confused and compounded by the division of the island. It's also confused by our proximity to England. You can't possibly – and don't even want to – jettison the whole English experience, but how to pick and choose what is valuable for us and what is health-giving for us, how to keep us from being a GAA⁵ republic, it's a very delicate tiptoeing enterprise. I think the possibilities for your generation are better in some kind of way.

FO'T: Doesn't the whole Field Day project then depend on political nationalism and on the achievement of a united Ireland?

BF: I don't think it should be read in those terms. I think it should lead to a cultural state, not a political state. And I think out of that cultural state, a possibility of a political state follows. That is always the sequence. It's very grandiose this, and I want to make notice of abdication quickly, but I think they are serious issues and big issues, and they are issues that exercise us all, the six of us [directors], very much. But you've also got to be very careful to retain some strong element of cynicism about the whole thing.

FO'T: That presumably is very much part of *The Communication Cord*.

BF: Oh, that's part of it. I want it to be seen in tandem with *Translations*.

FO'T: Doesn't the whole enterprise of Field Day, though, beg the question of the power of art to affect society? I mean theatre is by and large peripheral, it's just treated as another social event.

BF: But it's got to succeed on that level. It's got to succeed on that level first. You can't suddenly say, 'To hell with all those middle-class fur coat people – fuck them out; we want the great unwashed.' You've got to take the material you have. There are other theatre groups who are into something else. If you're into agitprop or if you're into political theatre or if you're into street theatre – that's your enterprise. We're not into that kind of enterprise. I think what we're saying is: we'll go to the people who are there but we'll talk to them in a certain kind of way. You know, we're living with what we have. We're trying to talk to them in a different voice and we're trying to adjust them to our way of thinking.

FO'T: Doesn't the health of the whole thing, though, need an audience which is capable of change? Do you believe that the current theatre audience which tends to be middle-class and to have certain expectations is capable of being adjusted in this way?

BF: That's truer in Dublin than it is elsewhere, because there is a theatrical experience and a theatrical tradition in Dublin. There is no theatrical tradition in Belfast. There's very little anywhere else around the country. And this is in some kind of a way why it's nice and cosy to say, you know, we get such great response when we're doing the one-night stands. That's nice and easy. But in some way it's true on a different kind of level – that these people watch you very carefully. They watch you almost as if we were cattle being paraded around on a fair day. They watch us with that kind of cool assessment. And they're listening. I think they hear things in theatre because they haven't been indoctrinated in the way a metropolitan audience is. They hear different sounds in a play. They are great audiences in a different kind of way to a Dublin theatre audience. Going back to your question – you say, you're speaking to the same people. We're not in fact speaking to the same people apart from Dublin. This is one of the reasons why we're happy to go to Dublin and play for a week, and the only reason we would go and play for four weeks would be to make money which would fund us the next time around. It's not a question at all of turning your back on the capital city but we're into something else, I think.

FO'T: *The Communication Cord* is probably the most formally conservative play you've done for a long time. How important is a sense of form to you? There are people who would say that for a writer to be focusing so strongly, as you are, on the tools of his own trade, on language, is in some way incestuous considering the urgency of so many things that need to be said.

BF: Do you think it's a valid criticism?

FO'T: I don't think so personally because I think the problem of language is a profoundly political one in itself.

BF: Particularly politics on this island, where you listen to a cabinet minister from Dublin and he's speaking such a debased language that you wonder how in God's name can this man have anything to do with your life at all. I think that is how the political problem of this island is going to be solved. It's going to be solved by language in some kind of way. Not only the language of negotiations across the table. It's going to be solved by the recognition of what language means for us on this island. Whether we're speaking the kind of English that I would use, or whether we're using the kind of English that Enoch Powell would use. Because we are in fact talking about accommodation or marrying of two cultures here, which are ostensibly speaking the same language but which in fact aren't.

FO'T: Your own work as a writer is very much bound up with that clash of cultures, and there's the old cliché about times of trouble leading to a flowering of literature. Do you ever feel that you're feeding off the suffering here?

BF: We're looting the shop when it's burning, you mean? I mean, this is often said, and it's said of all the Northern poets particularly. I don't know. The experience is there, it's available. We didn't create it, and it has coloured all our lives and adjusted all our stances in some way. What the hell can we do but look at it?

Making a Reply to the Criticisms of *Translations* by J. H. Andrews (1983)

. . . I feel very lucky that I have been corrected only for using a few misplaced bayonets and for suggesting that British soldiers might have been employed to evict peasants. I felt that I had merited more reprimands than that.

Perhaps the simplest thing might be if I were to tell you, very briefly, something about the genesis of *Translations* and the notions I was flirting with before I came across [J. H. Andrews's] *A Paper Landscape* [Oxford: Clarendon Press, 1975] and how those notions were adjusted and how they evolved after reading that book.

At any given time every playwright has half a dozen ideas that drift in and out of his awareness. For about five years before I wrote *Translations* there were various nebulous notions that kept visiting me and leaving me: a play set in the nineteenth century, somewhere between the Act of Union [1801] and the Great Famine [1845–47]; a play about Daniel O'Connell and Catholic emancipation; a play about colonialism; and the one constant – a play about the death of the Irish language and the acquisition of English and the profound effects that that change-over would have on a people. These were the kinds of shadowy notions that visited me and left me. But even when they had left me, from some of those ideas I was still getting persistent and strong signals.

During that same period (I am talking about the period prior to attempting the play that became *Translations*) I made two accidental discoveries. One, I learned that a great-great-grandfather of mine, a man called McCabe from County Mayo, had been a hedge-schoolmaster, had left Mayo and had come up to Donegal where he settled; and it was whispered in the family that he was fond of a drop. That discovery sent me into reading about the hedge-schools in this country and particularly to [P. J.] Dowling's *The Hedge Schools of Ireland* [1935, revised 1968]. And the sec-

ond casual discovery I made at that time – this was really shame-
ful but I hadn't known it until that point – was that directly across
the River Foyle from where I live in Muff is a place called Magilligan and it was at Magilligan that the first trigonometrical base for
the ordnance survey was set up in 1828; and the man in charge of
that survey was Colonel Colby. And that discovery sent me to
Colby's book, *A Memoir of the City and the North-West Liberties
of Londonderry* [1837], a very rich and wonderful book. And
about the same time, too, as I made these discoveries, I began
reading the letters that John O'Donovan wrote when he was
working for the Ordnance Survey. He was surveying in Donegal
in 1835, 'taking place-names' – if I may quote approximately
from the play – 'that were riddled with confusion and standardiz-
ing those names as accurately and as sensitively as he could'
[1981, p. 43]. So that was the general background: fugitive
notions of a play about language, and simultaneously an incipient
interest in the ordnance survey itself and particularly in the ortho-
graphical pursuits and torments of John O'Donovan.

Then in 1976 I came across *A Paper Landscape*. And suddenly
here was the confluence – the aggregate – of all those notions that
had been visiting me over the previous years: the first half of the
nineteenth century: an aspect of colonialism; the death of the Irish
language and the acquisition of English. Here were all the elements I had been dallying with, all synthesized in one very comprehensive and precise text. Here was the perfect metaphor to
accommodate and realize all those shadowy notions – map-making. Now, it seemed to me, all I had to do was dramatize *A Paper
Landscape*. (It seemed an excess of good luck that even Daniel
O'Connell appeared in the book: 'A newspaper report of 1828
drew the idyllic picture of how the people of Glenomara, County
Clare, had helped the engineers to build a trigonometrical station,
climbing their mountain in a great crowd with flutes, pipes and
violins, and young women bearing laurel leaves; although they
insisted on naming the station "O'Connell's Tower".' Even the
detail of the young woman bearing laurel leaves had the reassuring echoes of Ibsen.)

I plunged straight off into a play about Colonel Colby, the
prime mover in the ordnance survey of this island. Writers sometimes allow themselves to be seduced by extraneous and alto-

gether trivial elements in their material; and what fascinated me about Colby was not that he masterminded the huge task of mapping this country for the best part of forty years but the fact that he had one hand. That Oedipal detail seemed crucial to me, mesmerized me. And for many deluded months I pursued Colby and tried to make him amenable to my fictional notion of him. The attempt failed. And Colby appears in *Translations* as a minor character called Captain Lancey.

When Colby escaped me, I turned my attention to John O'Donovan. And just as I allowed myself to be misled by Colby's missing hand, so now I indulged in an even more bizarre and dangerous speculation: I read into O'Donovan's exemplary career as a scholar and orthographer the actions and perfidy of a quisling. (The only excuse I can offer for this short-lived delusion is that the political situation in the North was particularly tense about that time.) Thankfully, that absurd and cruel reading of O'Donovan's character was short-lived. But it soured a full tasting of the man. And O'Donovan appears in the play as a character called Owen.

I now went back to the earlier notion of trying to do something with O'Connell. But he had no part in the map-making metaphor, to which I was now wedded. And in my disappointment poor O'Connell gets only a few lines in the play.

Finally and sensibly I abandoned the idea of trying to dramatize *A Paper Landscape* and embarked on a play about a drunken hedge-schoolmaster.

Now that I meet Professor Andrews for the first time I want to thank him for providing me with that metaphor and to apologize to him for the tiny bruises inflicted on history in the play. He has pointed out the error of the bayonet.[1] I would like to admit to a couple of other sins.[2] One is having Donegal renamed in 1833 when in fact the task was not undertaken until two years later. Another is calling one of the characters Yolland and placing him in Donegal in 1833 when in fact the actual Yolland did not join the survey department until 1838. But I am sure that Professor Andrews will agree that the imperatives of fiction are as exacting as the imperatives of cartography and historiography.

Writing an historical play may bestow certain advantages but it also imposes particular responsibilities. The apparent advantages are the established historical facts or at least the received historical ideas in which the work is rooted and which give it its apparent familiarity and accessibility. The concomitant responsibility is to acknowledge those facts or ideas but not to defer to them. Drama is first a fiction, with the authority of fiction. You don't go to *Macbeth* for history.

Thomas Heywood, a contemporary of Shakespeare, defined historical plays – or chronicle plays, as he called them – in these terms:

> Chronicle plays are written with this aim and carried with this method: to teach the subjects obedience to their king; to show the people the untimely ends of such as have moved tumults, commotions and insurrections; to present them with the flourishing estate of such as live in obedience, exhorting them to allegiance, dehorting them from all traitorous and felonious stratagems.

If we accept that definition of an historical play, *Translations* is a total failure. But viewed from a different age – and maybe a different island – perhaps some merit can be found in it.

Important Places: A Preface to Charles McGlinchey's *The Last of the Name* (1986)

On a couple of evenings every week during the winters of the late 1940s and early 1950s Patrick Kavanagh, principal teacher in Gaddyduff National School in the village of Clonmany, County Donegal, visited Charles McGlinchey, weaver and tailor, in his home in Cluainte a few miles away. McGlinchey was then in his late eighties and early nineties and, in the way of old men and women who have an intuitive sense of themselves and whose span is running out, he was eager to talk about his life and times. Master Kavanagh wrote down in longhand what his friend had to tell, because Kavanagh, in the tradition of rural schoolmasters who have a cultivated sense of their locus, knew that the stories he was being told were important. Each man complemented and fulfilled the other. The result of that partnership is this book.

McGlinchey's memoir is a chronicle of a period of profound transition in this island and he himself is a Janus figure facing in two directions. The historian or sociologist can arbitrarily choose almost any period in the history of a society and demonstrate that at that particular time significant changes took place in the life of a people. If the chosen period were McGlinchey's life (1861–1954) attention would rightly focus on issues like Home Rule and the land wars, the rise and fall of Parnell, the Rising in 1916, two world wars, the atomic bomb. McGlinchey does not mention even one of these events. They are overlooked in a manner that is almost Olympian. They do not merit his notice. But by his concentration on the everyday, the domestic, the familiar, the nuance of a phrase, the tiny adjustment to a local ritual, the momentous daily trivia of the world of his parish, he does give us an exact and lucid picture of profound transition: a rural community in the process of shedding the last vestiges of a Gaelic past and of an old Christianity that still cohabited with an older paganism, and of that community coming to uneasy accommodation with the world of today, 'the buses, the cars, the silk stockings'.

The history of his life is uncomplicated. He was born in the Meentiagh Glen, a remote and mountainy place that lies between Ballyliffin and Buncrana on the western side of the Inishowen peninsula. His father before him was a weaver and tailor. He had four brothers and two sisters. He had very little schooling but spoke Irish and English and could read both. (On two uncharacteristic occasions in the memoir, probably to impress the transcribing schoolmaster, he bursts into bog Latin.) He never married. He outlived all his family and when he died in his ninety-fourth year he was buried in the family plot. 'And after my day the grave will not be opened again, for I'm the last of the name.'

Anything that was not rooted in the daily life of the glen did not merit his observation. He tells us almost as an aside of the only two occasions when he ventured out of the parish. Once when he was 'drawing up on thirty' he went to Berwick-on-Tweed in Scotland for the harvest season. He makes no comment at all on that excursion apart from the sparse information that the work was 'shearing and lifting corn and the wages were £1 a week with my keep. I was given a blanket and slept on straw in the barn.' His second recorded journey was to the Eucharistic Congress in Dublin in 1932. Indeed he refers to that occasion not as a spiritual pilgrimage but as an illustration of how long a raked fire will keep lit: 'I raked the fire myself one Saturday morning in 1932, and went to the Eucharistic Congress in Dublin and didn't get back till Monday evening. The fire was living in the rakings all the time.'

The manuscript that Master Kavanagh's son Desmond gave to me to edit was frequently meandering and repetitive, and one of the many rigours I imposed on it to give it its present shape was to fragment that flowing, conversational speech into chapters and to give those chapters titles. (Imposing a literary shape on material that derives its character and vigour from a different form is an uncertain enterprise. It can be justified, I hope, in that it makes material like this available to a general public.) McGlinchey, reared on the stories of Fionn and Oisín and the Fianna – 'stories so long that they wouldn't be finished at bedtime, so the old man would carry on the next night where he left off' – lives uneasily under that kind of regimentation. His remembering style resists

such external structuring; a conversation has a right to be meandering and repetitive – maybe for emphasis, maybe for the music
of the speech, maybe just because the old man is forgetful.

But despite my formal disciplining there are some themes that
keep recurring throughout the text. Religion is a preoccupation,
and the behaviour of Catholic priests and Protestant ministers, and
the mixed marriage of the old pagan practices with the new Christian dogmas, and the power of the shaman's curse. McGlinchey was
a Catholic but his Catholicism is closer to the eighteenth century
than to the twentieth. He likes the mendicant friars with their rau-
cous drinking and their 'breezy' ways and their open hearts. He is
less happy with Father Shiels who in 1820 built a big house for himself, and 'in order to make up the farm seven families had to be
evicted. He helped at the evicting himself, too. I heard that he
evicted one family after he had said Mass and before he took his
breakfast; and he even carried out a cradle with an infant in it and
left it on the street. The old people didn't want to talk about it.' The
story is told in a flat voice, the same tone he uses to describe the
death in 1703 of Colonel McNeill, the notorious landlord – land-
lords are another preoccupation. 'Things got so bad at the finish-up
that some of the Ardagh men attacked McNeill one night at a place
called Gallach in Annagh Hill, and felled him with a stone on the
head, and Eoin Airis McCole castrated him with an old hook. His
henchmen carried him home, and he lay for days before he died.'

The poet Patrick Kavanagh begins 'Epic' with the lines:

I have lived in important places, times
When great events were decided, who owned
That half a rood of rock, a no-man's land
Surrounded by our pitchfork-armed claims.

Meentiagh Glen is an important place, not of itself but because
an astute man observed it and his observations bestowed an
importance on it, elicited its importance from it. And that simulta-
neous bestowing and eliciting is the act of art. *The Last of the
Name* is the work of an artist.

When I was working on this manuscript I received invaluable help
from Conal Byrne who knew Charles McGlinchey and who knows
the whole of Inishowen fondly and intimately. Conal Byrne is in the
mould of Master Kavanagh – schoolmasters with a great *pietas*.

In Interview with Laurence Finnegan (1986)

Laurence Finnegan: Firstly, starting with the plays, when did you start writing? How did you get involved with drama?

Brian Friel: I began writing short stories and – at a point when I recognized that this was a much more complex form and more delicate form than I knew when I was blundering to it, at that stage I stopped stories and began writing some radio plays and then met up with Tyrone Guthrie who was a Monaghan man originally. Guthrie, at that point – 1962 to '63 – was building his theatre at Minneapolis. I went out at that point to stay there for five or six months or something like that.

I had written two stage plays before that but that was a kind of lift-off and it was the first experience. I never had anything to do with amateur theatre. It's a pursuit that I don't have much interest in now.

LF: So would you see Guthrie as the major influence at that point?

BF: I'm never quite sure what the influences are, you know, but he was some kind of levelling influence as much as a signposting influence.

LF: The play that brought, most immediately, your name to the headlines was *Philadelphia*, which in many ways was also an unusual play. Was that a Guthrie type of influence?

BF: It probably was, because he was a very large – in all kinds of ways an expansive – man. He was the kind of man who gave you the courage to take formal gambles and technical gambles on the stage, and I can't think of it in those terms now but I suppose at that stage it was a gamble – a risky enterprise in terms of form. It's a play I'm really off now: I've no interest in it now.

LF: Eugene McCabe, who also did one of these interviews, mentioned in the course of it that he had found himself not involved in the Northern thing, and he quoted you as saying, 'You know, we've got to be involved.' Was there a point where you made a conscious decision about this?

BF: There still isn't a conscious decision, and if Eugene said I said that to him I'm sure it's true but, you know, I certainly wouldn't say it to anybody now. The problem is the conflict between the public self, the social self and the artistic self, and the artistic self demands privacy, demands secrecy, it demands introversion; the social sense demands something altogether different. The public sense demands effort, engagement; it demands things like the cause of *patria* and this is the constant conflict that I think no Northerners can resolve properly. Someone like Heaney succeeds in tiptoeing through the minefield very skilfully. Some of the rest of us have plunged in and I think with some regret now perhaps.

LF: Does the artist have a role, should the artist be out there making statements about what's happening in the public sector?

BF: This is the perennial problem. Auden says that a poem doesn't affect the slightest thing in the public domain: 'For poetry makes nothing happen.' It's all very well to articulate that theory but, you know, we are also made up of the impure genes of the social self and they make demands on you; there are demands which have got to be resisted – the demands of the tribe. The demands of the tribe in this part of Ireland are enormous.

LF: And would you see those as negative in a sense?

BF: I think there's a conflict. I'm not saying which is positive and which is negative. I think in some kind of way they are equal and opposite stresses. I'm not identifying one as positive or another as evil or malign or benign – I'm just saying that they are positive and equal – they are almost physical forces in the sense of physics. They are equal and opposite forces pulling in two different directions and I think, if you can find the ideal confluence where those two forces can function nobly and honourably, with nobility and honour to both of them, then there is a possibility of producing art, but I think the chance of producing art with those kinds of pulls is enormously difficult.

LF: And yet one play that I personally find myself going over again and again is *Translations:* it's not a political play as such but it is a lot about dealing with cultural change. Were you very conscious of that at the time?

BF: Well, it was the kind of founding play of this enterprise that we're involved in now – this Field Day enterprise. I don't know, is that to its credit or not? I suppose it is. I don't think *Translations* is a political play – I think it has to do more directly with almost blatant cultural enterprises. I don't really have much to say about it.

LF: I was thinking here in terms of a national identity, and looking at Owen and his readiness to move forward as a figure of progress and re-name the townlands, and that other culture that was steeped in the Gaelic language and the Latin and Greek, a very sophisticated, superior culture . . .

BF: But if anything was achieved there, all that was achieved were the demarcation lines. I mean, the play made no attempt to offer any kind of solution. All it did was acknowledge the ground plan of distinction and difference. *The Freedom of the City* was a more reckless play and a much more ill-considered play because it was written out of the kind of anger at the Bloody Sunday events in Derry. I don't say I regret it but I certainly wouldn't do it now.

LF: In Irish drama do you see the Irish writer as inhabiting a particularly Irish discourse?

BF: With whom?

LF: With his own people – with Ireland – or would you see it as being part of the mainline European movement?

BF: I think the discourse is primarily with yourself: it is always with yourself, and this is back again to the first of those two physical forces, and to maintain fealty to yourself, particularly in a place like this, is an enormously difficult one and I think the moment you begin huckstering in the public domain and huckstering with the public language, and with the public political discourse, then you are in danger because you are endangering the discourse with oneself.

LF: So you see it, as you mentioned, as a very private business?

BF: I think it is always fundamentally and primarily an attempt to give some kind of structure to your own life and your own beliefs and your own confusions. You simply choose a particular medium like theatre because you believe that perhaps this may have some meaning and some validity for other people.

LF: Could you say a word about theatre? I mean, you started out writing short stories – why is theatre now your preferred medium?

BF: I'm attracted to everything that's vulgar and cheap about theatre, and a lot of theatre is vulgar and cheap. It's very attractive: it's quite easy but it's also attractive. To force an audience into a single receiving and perceptive unit is a very easy thing to do. It's like, if you are a conjuror you can do certain tricks – it's an easy thing to do if you have a certain minuscule talent for it – that's all it is. It's a very easy thing once you have forged those 500 disparate people into one receiving entity – it's a very easy thing to make them laugh, it's a very easy thing to make them cry, and those are all very tempting tricks to play and they are cheap tricks and they are vulgar tricks, you know? This is one of the strengths of [Thomas] Kilroy's *Double Cross,* you see.

LF: But is this central? If we look at the great dramatists – for example, Shakespeare used all the tricks in the book in many ways to get the audience with him, but . . .

BF: And then in desperation said, OK, *As You Like It,* you know.

LF: But isn't there a distinctive thing about the spoken word, moving action on through dialogue, that's very different from any other art form?

BF: There may be some difference. But there's common ground too. I mean, for example, what we have seen a return to on this island is poets reading publicly. Which is in fact a kind of theatre; it's a voice on the stage saying, 'Come together and listen to me and I will forge you into one entity and I can talk to you then almost as an individual.'

LF: Would you like to say a word about your own reaction to *Philadelphia, Here I Come!* if it were staged now.

BF: I really have no reaction – no, it's not that I don't want to. It's over twenty years ago.

LF: Do you find it ironic that it's now twenty years later that the Department of Education decides to put your play on the syllabus for the Leaving Certificate?

BF: Some kind of warning signal, that. Either you're spent or that you have been made part of the establishment and that you're really past it or something. It means you're aged, you know, that's what it means, and it means that you're no longer a chancer, that you no longer do anything that's going to embarrass the establishment. But as a play I don't have any interest in it at all.

LF: Would you be prepared to say a word or two about what I feel is this ideological crisis facing us – which I think you have explored in some ways in your work – as a nation? Do you think the artist has something to say in helping a people define who they are, what they are?

BF: He has only got to find who he is and what *he* is and the structure of his own life. If he can do that in some kind of way then he may be arrogant enough to attempt to share that with somebody else. But I think that is his only function. I mean, I don't believe with Mr Gay Byrne that the country's banjaxed.

LF: Nor do I. Yet if we were to look at the kind of ideology that has informed Irish education – to come back to this just for a moment – and indeed Irish society through the 1930s, the '40s, the '50s, and up to the time of Ireland joining the EEC, we largely saw ourselves as nationalist, Catholic, or rural. We glorified these things and the heroes of 1916, and I think that certainly in the South these have been tarnished – through first of all the prosperity that came along, the materialism that came along with the EEC. Also, I think that the certainty of our identity as a Catholic nation – the faith of our fathers – is certainly going but is it being replaced by anything? And has the artist, or can the creative writer, make a contribution to helping the people define who they are? You don't have this problem in the North as much, I think, actually. What do you think?

BF: Oh, we have the problem, the problem is accentuated in the North, I think. The very things that you identify with the Free State – as we call it here – are seen here writ large, in great capitals. In fact, this is part of this Field Day enterprise: in some kind of way it's the coming together of six people who believe individually that by expressing, let's say with some artistic grace or skill or profundity or whatever, their own response, their own lives here in this condition up here, perhaps there is a redefinition of the kind of mythological Minotaurs that are dominating our lives here.

LF: But it would seem that Catholic nationalists in the North have a goal and a very strong sense of identity in a way which people, to use your phrase, in the Free State, have lost, isn't that so?

BF: I'm not sure. Maybe it's kind of an identity. I'm not sure it is, I think it's more kind of cohesion, that's all it is, but I don't think it has any permanent or any deep cultural binding force. I think it is simply some kind of cohesion and it is of no more profundity than belonging, for example, to, say, the Elks in America or the Shriners or whatever.

LF: Yes, except you can't leave it, can you? You can't opt out really?

BF: You can, but if you do you're in a wilderness and that's the problem.

LF: As a writer, how do you feel about what television is doing and what the kind of mass pop culture is doing to our youth? Are we losing them to something which is really a prefabricated commercial enterprise?

BF: I'm sure that's a very real issue. It's the kind of question I barely understand, you know. I know what you're saying but it's not a question that impinges on me in any kind of way.

LF: What are your own concerns then, your own concerns now as a writer?

BF: Well, they are always personal and private concerns. I haven't written a play for five years. I may never write another play. That induces a kind of panic. It also provokes a kind of peace. These are the kinds of questions that activate me, concern me. The Northern situation concerns me – profoundly – and exercises me far beyond its worth, really, because it is in fact only another accident of life.

LF: Which we're all caught up in though.

BF: Yeah.

LF: It is our lives. It's highly localized, isn't it?

BF: What happens in the Free State – I'm used to calling it the Free State because that's how it is used here – somehow, for some reason, although I live there, concerns me less.

LF: Your soul is here.

BF: Yeah.

LF: What do you think is going to happen?

BF: I think it's going to blow up.

LF: And there's going to be a lot of bloodshed.

BF: I was talking to a neighbour of mine yesterday who said Thatcher will back down and I said I'd put a fiver bet on she wouldn't. He said she will and she'll do it today, Thursday, and she spoke again today and she won't. If she doesn't, not for the first time – for the second time – you'll have loyalists in confrontation with their Crown.

LF: You don't feel at all at ease about telling me about your own schoolteaching. You did teach English, didn't you?

BF: I taught with the Christian Brothers for seven years and they were a very blunt instrument, I think, in education. That was in what would now be called an intermediate school in Derry, in the Bogside. Then I left that and taught for three years in a primary school which was tremendous: it was kind of an epiphany, you know. It was something different. It wasn't the kind of Christian Brothers stuff. And then I packed it in.

LF: At that stage you had already started to write?

BF: I had been writing at that point, yeah, for some time.

LF: Did you go to the Christian Brothers yourself?

BF: No.

LF: Did you go to 'the ranch', as they used to call it, in Belfast? [St Joseph's College of Education]

BF: I was at the ranch, yeah – it was another blunt instrument. It was a crude place. I don't know what it's like now.

LF: You have no desire whatever, I presume, to go back to teaching?

BF: No, I liked teaching, in spite of the difficulties. I was very young when I taught in the Christian Brothers. But I miss the teaching – I mean, I miss the companionship of it. I miss the children too. I certainly missed the primary teaching a lot for a long time but I wouldn't be competent to do it now. It's been twenty-five years or more, now . . .

LF: Would you be interested, or do you think it's important, in seeing drama taught in the schools as a separate subject?

BF: The only drama I have any interest in is the professional theatre which is the only theatre I have any experience of. I really have some kind of antipathy to amateur drama. I mean, this is probably the only country in Europe where amateur drama is treated at the same level as professional drama and the same critical language is used in describing it. The same reviewers review amateur productions and professional productions. There is no discrimination in the language they use and I find this very difficult. If we want to have amateur teachers, let's have them; if we want to have amateur doctors, let's have them.

LF: I had the feeling that amateur drama in country towns gave a sense of cohesion, again, a sense of wonder to young people growing up that just doesn't exist today. I remember the local plays and having my first interest in theatre arising out of amateur drama. So isn't it important?

BF: It's a blank spot I have – you know.

LF: You were probably never involved in it yourself – you went straight into professional theatre?

BF: That's right. I was never involved in it.

LF: Do you see drama, the medium, as going through major changes at the moment in terms of the way it is communicating itself?

BF: I think theatre has moved into a very dangerous position for itself. It has now become very, very expensive and very dependent on funding from state and private corporations, and I think this is a very bad thing for theatre because it's actually determining to some extent the kind of theatre that is written. Nobody nowadays can write a play with fifteen characters because it's too expensive – you can't put it on. You go down to ten characters and it's still too expensive. You end up doing monologues, one-man shows. You end up with two characters and one set, and this is very wrong. It's also wrong for actors and directors and everybody else. I think theatre has got to go back to the days when it was rogues and vagabonds and travelling and so on.

LF: And Field Day is going to do it, isn't it?

BF: We have our cosseted actors, you know, who get their state money and get their subsistence and so on, and the designers and the directors and everybody else. The finances are determining the kind of drama and therefore are determining what's being said on stages. This is the problem.

LF: I was thinking more of the theatre, you know when I said 'changes' – the Theatre of the Absurd – or the experimental theatre that you get in New York or in West Germany – a move away from language. Do you see changes of that kind?

BF: Well, we're inclined always to look towards England for our models in theatre, and I think we should be looking towards America. I think English theatre is spent now. Again, for some of the economic reasons I talked about. The dominant leaders of the English theatre, a lot of them, are Marxist, and because of this obsession with Marxism I think theatre is being boxed into a cultural corner. As the country itself is becoming more and more depleted in all kinds of ways, I suppose the theatre becomes less exploratory and less dangerous. Their theatre now in England is a celebratory theatre because you have the National Theatre in London and the RSC, which are two celebratory theatres, celebrating a tradition.

LF: How do you see the Abbey?

BF: No reason for it at all, no reason for its existence. This is no comment on what's happening there. I'm merely saying that I don't understand what a national theatre is any more. I don't understand the need for a national theatre because it would imply that there is some kind of a national voice and it comes back to the individual voice. I think that certainly you don't need a national theatre any more than you need a national airline.

LF: Do I hear you in some way also saying that you're not entirely in favour of subsidized arts at all, subsidized theatre?

BF: Well, I'm just saying that it's now got to the point where in the subsidized theatre what matters is the guarantee. Something profoundly wrong there.

LF: So, theatre you see as primarily entertaining? It should start out by packing people in?

BF: Oh, no, I didn't say that, no. I'm saying, if it *does* that, I mean that's probably more a comment on audiences rather than on what's offered to them.

LF: But, if we educate an audience, surely good theatre, or good art or good poetry or good paintings, or good music or whatever, must produce a culture that is aware at a deeper level of meaning than a culture that is tuned into pop or the like?

BF: You have a much more acute and much more lucid sense of a culture than I have. For you, culture is . . .

LF: A high culture, if I can use that word.

BF: Even a high culture – you see it almost . . . You can almost look at it the way you can look at, say, a satellite map of atmospheric conditions. I mean, you can look down on Ireland and say there is a large dense cloud of high culture moving towards the country or moving away from the country, and it's as explicit and as homogeneous as that for you, it seems. I don't know what a culture is, really.

LF: The difference I am making is what I would call a culture which is authentic, which originates within the people and is coming from their own needs – whether it's a pygmy tribe in Australia or whether it is an Irish group of people living in Athenry.

BF: But all you're doing is defining the distinctions between what you call a culture in one place and a culture in another place.

LF: I'm not saying that one is more valuable necessarily than the other at all. When I talk about a commercialized culture I'm talking about basically *Dynasty* and *Dallas* and how all over Ireland these are fed upon.

BF: Maybe those are simply modern myths that require a specific interpretation. What's the difference between J. R. and Finn Mac Cool? I don't know.

LF: That's what I'd love to know – is there a difference?

BF: Perhaps not, as long as you've got the capacity to interpret the myth and as long as you have the capacity to dismantle it and find out what the relevance of that is to yourself but not to your Irishness – just to yourself. You know what I'm saying?

LF: Yes, I do.

BF: I'm not asking whether it's relevant or instructive or informative for your Irishness. I'm just saying that it might tell you something about yourself, and perhaps the mythology of *Dallas* is as authentic a mythology as the mythology of the Red Branch.

LF: Yes, except that Cuchulainn – one could suggest as a myth – was a heroic myth, and it was the myth of great deeds and sacrifice and the nobility of service to the King, to Maeve, to Ulster, where the J. R. mythology is about consumerism, written large, and power.

BF: But that's also very important – the American dream, isn't it? That is surely the most informative myth in the American continent, isn't it? The dream of success, the dream of achievement, the dream of fulfilment through these materials. It is not an acceptable myth for us because we pay lip service to some kind of spiritual values.

LF: Do we still?

BF: We do. I mean, you say you want a culture that in some way speaks to something, and you made the gesture of pointing towards your soul, if that's where it resides. But maybe that's a kind of holiness too – perhaps.

LF: I feel we like to think we are a spiritual people and I think we're even giving up on the pretence of that.

BF: Well, we're a spiritual people to the extent, I suppose, that our language is shot through with the language of spirituality and the language of the other world and the language of otherness, and that language is easily available to us. But my children, for example, have great difficulty with the kind of language that I can use and perhaps that you can use because they don't know the terminology. I think there's a loss there, particularly in this society, when the young aren't totally conversant with the subtleties of language. I'm not concerned about the spiritual loss, that's less important; but the linguistic loss is important.

LF: I'd like you to come back a little bit maybe to some thoughts about this teaching business and education. Did you do Shakespeare at school? Looking back on it: did it mean anything to you?

BF: I don't remember – I don't think so. I don't remember.

LF: I remember learning chunks of *Julius Caesar* . . .

BF: No, I must say, I have a slightly more lucid memory of doing poetry at school and not finding anything in it at all. I remember doing Keats and Shelley and Wordsworth and Milton and finding nothing in it . . .

LF: But how much of that was because it's not amenable to children at that age?

BF: I don't know the answer to that . . .

LF: But you were a teacher . . .

BF: I taught maths.

LF: Oh, you taught maths! I didn't know that.

BF: I taught maths for the Christian Brothers.

LF: You must be one of the first maths men to move into drama.

BF: It was a simple maths at that time. I was always a sort of step ahead of the posse.

LF: As a child – can I go back into this?

BF: No.

LF: You don't want to . . . You didn't write?

BF: I didn't write.

LF: But there must be some . . .

(*Noises from the street disrupt interview*)

BF: There's a nice image for you out there. You're looking for the culture of Ireland: there are the punks and the skinheads of Derry sitting, eating, lying against the cannon from the seventeenth century. (*Laughs*)

LF: These are the walls – you can walk . . .

BF: Right round them, yeah.

LF: Were there any Irish playwrights who influenced you?

BF: There are a couple of playwrights I think are fascinating and have never adequately been acknowledged in this country. I think

T. C. Murray is a major writer – for his time – it's a kind of limiting phrase but he was limited by the 1930s and '40s of Ireland that you were talking about earlier – certain freedoms of language and expression and technique were not available to him but within the confines of that he was a very big dramatist. T. C. Murray? You don't know him? He wrote *Autumn Fire* [1924] and *The Briery Gap* [1917] and plays like that. There's another man called George Fitzmaurice – do you know George Fitzmaurice? A Kerry man – a fascinating man whose father was a minister in Listowel, and a man that Yeats in some way muted and neutered because he was slightly jealous of him and wouldn't give him any encouragement, wouldn't produce him. These were two important men on *this* island.

LF: I haven't even seen them performed.

BF: The Abbey, years ago, did some Fitzmaurice and they did Murray too – they would have been done in the 1930s, '40s and '50s. They would be fairly close to the kind of thing that John B. Keane does – kind of folk drama but it's very sophisticated folk drama. Do you know of a Spanish dramatist called Lorca?

LF: Yes, I do.

BF: Fitzmaurice is very close to Lorca. Fitzmaurice has short plays – in fact, I think he must have been influenced by Lorca – I would imagine. Fantastic plays – the world of fantasy is his home.

LF: You said there, at one point, that you're not sure whether you'd write again?

BF: Five years is a long time to be immobile, you know.

LF: But you have been involved with theatre all that time?

BF: Yes, but that's . . . in many ways, peripheral.

Programme Note for *Making History* (1988)

Making History is a dramatic fiction that uses some actual and some imagined events in the life of Hugh O'Neill to make a story. I have tried to be objective and faithful – after my artistic fashion – to the empirical method. But when there was tension between historical 'fact' and the imperative of the fiction, I'm glad to say I kept faith with the narrative. For example, even though Mabel, Hugh's wife, died in 1591, it suited my story to keep her alive for another ten years. Part of me regrets taking these occasional liberties. But then I remind myself that history and fiction are related and comparable forms of discourse and that an historical text is a kind of literary artifact. And then I am grateful that these regrets were never inhibiting.[1]

'To give an accurate description of what has never happened is not merely the proper occupation of the historian, but the inalienable privilege of any man of arts and culture.'

Oscar Wilde, The Critic as Artist

Preface to *The London Vertigo* (1990)

The desire to metamorphose oneself, to change everything utterly
– name, beliefs, voice, loyalties, language, ambitions, even one's
appearance – secretly excites most people at some stage of their
lives, and is as old as Adam. It is an element in the dream that
charms young people into a career in acting. It is the private delir-
ium that middle-aged writers are especially vulnerable to: to oblit-
erate that whole past of botched and failed and embarrassing
work and to begin afresh and anonymously with a few simple
markings on a white sheet of paper. And of course the desire is a
delusion. There are no new beginnings with new identities, as
Cathal MacLochlainn [Charles Macklin], the eighteenth-century
actor and playwright, discovered. But his attempt at transmogrifi-
cation is interesting for two reasons. The first is that he set about
it with calculation and precocious acumen while he was still only
a boy, long before he knew the pain of failure as a writer or as an
actor. The second is that he pulled it off. Well, almost.

MacLochlainn was born some time during the last decade of
the seventeenth century in the townland of Gortanarin in the
parish of Cloncha in the Inishowen peninsula in the very north of
County Donegal. Various birth-years are offered – 1690, 1693,
1699. Even as an old man (he died in 1797 when he may have
been anything from ninety-eight to one hundred and seven) he
never attempted to clear up the confusion, perhaps because the
actor liked to be ageless, more likely because the writer preferred
the past to be blurred. His background was poor peasant, his religion Catholicism, his only language Irish. Very early in life he recognized that an Irish-speaking Catholic peasant from north
Donegal did not possess the very best qualifications for success in
eighteenth-century Ireland. He emigrated to England. He learned
English and spoke it with an English accent. He changed his name
to Charles Macklin. He invented a background of wealth and

land in County Down. He converted to Protestantism. And the metamorphosis brought abundant success. London and Macklin loved one another. Before he was thirty he had a considerable reputation as a budding playwright and a rising star on the English stage. He became a friend of Garrick and Edmund Burke and Henry Fielding, was smiled on by royalty, was celebrated by Alexander Pope after the poet had seen his Shylock ('This is the Jew / That Shakespeare drew'), became famous for his Macbeth and his Iago and his own hugely popular *Love à la Mode*.

He was in his sixties when he wrote his first play with an Irish theme, *The True-Born Irishman*, a satirical look at Irish Anglophiles; and one marvels at Macklin's ease and assurance in his new identity, so confident that he would now attempt to write out of a discarded persona. The play opened at the Crow Street Theatre, Dublin, on 14 May 1761. Perhaps predictably, Irish audiences received it warmly.

The plot is simple. Nancy O'Doherty, wife of Murrough O'Doherty (played by Macklin himself), a pompous and ponderous Dublin burgher, has been to London for the coronation of George the Third. During her brief visit she has been smitten by 'the London vertigo', a sudden and dizzy conviction that London is the very heart of style and wit and good fortune and excitement. When the play opens she has recently returned to dreary Murrough O'Doherty.

Macklin wants her to be an absurd and ludicrous figure. He achieves this – without a hint of irony, it would seem – by two devices: the lady, now ashamed of her Irish name, O'Doherty, has decided to call herself Mrs Diggerty; and she now speaks a patois in a posh accent that her husband can scarcely understand. 'London – Dublin – don't neem [name] them together!' she says. 'After London everything I set my eyes on here gives me the *ennui* and the *contre cure*. The streets are mean, the houses dirty, the people ridiculous. And the women! None of the *non chalance*, none of that *jenny-see-quee* we have in London. And everything sounds so strange here! [. . .] Even the very dogs when they bark, I swear they bark wit' a brogue!'[1]

O'Doherty, distressed by his wife's lunacy, enlists the help of her brother and together they hatch a plot to restore her to sanity and thorough Irishness. By a series of complicated and cruel manoeuvres Macklin has Mrs Diggerty cured of her vertigo, properly humiliated before her friends and reconciled to decent Dublin domesticity. Simultaneously, and almost certainly unwittingly, Macklin has written his own biography as comedy/farce.

Six years passed before he brought *The True-Born Irishman* to London. It opened in Covent Garden on 28 November 1767. Circumspect as ever, Macklin retitled the play *The Irish Fine Lady*, just in case the original title might have a hint of coat-trailing for his English audience. But the play did not travel. Whatever the reason, the night was a disaster. And when the curtain came down Macklin rushed on to the stage in panic. 'Ladies and gentlemen,' he pleaded, 'I am very sensible that there are several passages in this play which deserve to be reprobated and I assure you that they shall never offend your ears again.' One can almost hear the terrified voice and the clipped Donegal vowels. Later, when he had composed himself, he said to a friend, 'I believe the audience are right. There is a geography in humour as well as in morals, which I had previously not considered.' What he meant by a geography in humour is clear enough; a geography in morals is nicely ambiguous. Anyhow, *The Irish Fine Lady* was withdrawn after that one performance.

I have worked on Macklin's text with affection and respect. I have pruned his script vigorously, mainly by compressing his three acts into one and by reducing his cast of fourteen to a cast of five. (The missing nine appear only briefly in his Act 2 and Act 3 and he uses them not to energize his central theme but as contemporary stereotypes who make leisurely and amusing social comment on mid-eighteenth-century Ireland; in other words, to stroke his audience.) But I trust – I believe – I have done neither structural nor aesthetic damage to the script. And in excuse for my ruthless culling of his cast I plead the stern economics of late-twentieth-century theatre. Indeed, my hope is that a lean and less discursive text may be more attractive to theatre companies today and better suited to our impatient stage.[2]

My reason for renaming the play *The London Vertigo* is that this title both signposts the play's theme and hints at the fate the author himself so eagerly embraced.

This may not be Macklin's best play – *The Man of the World* or *Love à la Mode* claims that place. But it is a very considerable piece of work from an almost completely self-made man and it gave me pleasure to work on it – a kind of *comhar* or co-operation or companionship with a neighbouring playwright.

In Interview with Mel Gussow (1991)

Late on a summer's evening in London in 1987, Brian Friel walked along the Thames Embankment with Tom Kilroy. The two playwrights had just left Britain's National Theatre, where they had seen Friel's dramatization of Turgenev's *Fathers and Sons*. As they passed homeless men and women curled up in doorways and trash-filled alleys, the writers speculated about the lives of these unfortunate people. Friel said that he had two maiden aunts who ended up like that – destitute and abandoned in London. Just before World War II, they had suddenly left the family home in the tiny village of Glenties in Ireland, and never returned. Caught up by the story, Kilroy suggested Friel write a play about it.

Back in Ireland, Friel took his friend's advice. It was in fact an idea that had been lodged deep in his memory bank – his remembrances of childhood summers spent with his mother and her sisters at his grandparents' house. For several years he had been trying to overcome a severe case of writer's block, but as he began to write, the play flowed freely. As *Dancing at Lughnasa* (pronounced *Loo*-na-sa, as in lunacy) evolved, it became the story of five sisters, all of them unmarried and living together, each stranded with an unrealized dream. The play is dedicated 'in memory of those five brave Glenties women', and 'out of piety' for his mother and her sisters, each of the characters bears the first name of the real-life model on whom she is based.

In the play, as in other of his works, Friel uses autobiography as a taking-off point for art with a far more universally relevant purpose. Probing his life for ideas, he becomes 'the miner and the mined'. *Dancing at Lughnasa* deals with characteristic Friel themes (dispossession, dreams of departure, lost illusions) and also – a new theme for the playwright – the Dionysiac side of even the most religious and outwardly repressed people, as exemplified by the desire of the sisters to dance at the annual harvest fair of Lughnasa, dedicated to the pagan god, Lugh.

In a surging *coup de théâtre*, the women create a spontaneous revel – not at Lughnasa but in their rustic home. Carried aloft by the beauty and the frenzy of the dance, theatre-goers also share a moment of ecstasy. The play concludes with a linguistic refrain of the earlier choreographic image. The character who stands in for the playwright says, 'There is one memory of that Lughnasa time that visits me most often.' Music of the 1930s 'drifts in from somewhere far away – a mirage of sound – a dream music that is both heard and imagined . . . When I remember it, I think of it as dancing . . . Dancing as if language had surrendered to movement – as if this ritual, this wordless ceremony, was now the way to speak, to whisper private and sacred things.'

Even before it opens at the Plymouth Theatre on 24 October, *Dancing at Lughnasa* has become Friel's greatest success, the capstone to date of a career that has produced more than twenty plays. In its prior engagements at Dublin's Abbey Theatre and in London, the play earned critical acclaim and an Olivier Award as best play of the season. It is the first new Irish play to achieve such wide popularity in England.

With its rueful and deeply compassionate family portrait and its provocative commentary on crosscurrents of paganism and Christianity, the play adds lustre to the playwright's ascendant reputation. With the death of Samuel Beckett [in 1989], he is Ireland's finest living playwright (his most accomplished peers are Hugh Leonard and Thomas Murphy). The author of *Philadelphia, Here I Come!*, *Aristocrats*, *Faith Healer*, *Translations* and *Dancing at Lughnasa*, Friel is at sixty-two very much in his prime, a writer on a level with Sean O'Casey and John Millington Synge.

Joe Dowling, who has directed plays by all three playwrights, says that in Friel's work, 'lives unfold before you', offering 'revelation within revelation'. He continues: 'I don't know of any other playwright in the English language who will go out on a limb as often as he does. He is the one who has most consistently over the last twenty-five years reflected the changes in Ireland.'

Lughnasa and almost all his other plays take place in Ballybeg, a mythical town in Donegal invented by Friel. In Gaelic, it is *baile beag*, and literally means small town. For Friel, it is a Ballybeg of

the mind. While he denies it has the specificity of Faulkner's Yok-
napatawpha, it is a microcosm of rural Ireland, and, by inference,
it represents small towns around the world.

Though he has occasionally written a play with an urban setting, his artistic home is Ballybeg. For this and other reasons, he is
often compared with Chekhov. Besides the fact that both are
short-story writers as well as playwrights, they share an empathy
for those who are trapped in seemingly ordinary lives and for the
importance of a provincial place as an adjunct of character. There
are societal changes in the background, but the people remain
land-locked within their emotional environment.

In *Lughnasa*, *Philadelphia* and other plays, the author stands
within and outside the narrative, commenting sardonically on
what in other hands might be regarded as nostalgia. Stylistically
he moves away from naturalism, employing striking theatrical
devices to shed a more intense light on his subject. In *Lughnasa*,
the artist as a boy is played by an adult actor, who becomes a kind
of overseer of the family history.

The plays take place at homecomings and leavings, reunions
and preludes to exile. Old worlds dissolve and traditional values
are questioned. Language is of the utmost concern – not simply
the lyrical language that elevates his plays, but in his commentary
on communication. He illustrates the power of things spoken and
unspoken, language as both divider and bridge.

Friel's plays are not nearly as simple as they might seem (including his few less successful satires and farces). At his best, he creates an intricately interwoven tapestry of character, atmosphere
and ideas. It is the kind of work that theatre-goers enjoy and academics love to sink their theses into. As with other artists, Friel
prefers to let his work speak for itself. He is reluctant to analyse it
or himself. As one friend says, trying to capture Friel is like 'shifting smoke with a pitchfork'.

He has followed his own private course to what has turned out
to be a rather public career. To be an artist in his country is to be
political, and, living all his life near the border of Northern Ireland, he keeps a foot in each of Ireland's two worlds. For a time,
at the invitation of the president of Ireland, he served in the Irish
Senate, the first writer since Yeats to be so honoured. As a public
official, he hardly said a word. But he has discoursed in his work,

addressing significant issues, including, in *Translations*, the historic crushing of Irish language and culture by the English.

Because of his closeness to Northern Ireland, some people assume that he is actively anti-British. Politics in Ireland is 'a muddy issue', he says. 'I do think the problem will always be exacerbated as long as England is in the country. But if England were to go tomorrow morning, that wouldn't solve it. We still have got to find a *modus vivendi* for ourselves within the country.'

To questions of a more personal or artistic nature, he can offer the tersest response but, after dodging, he will encourage the questioner by saying, 'Persist! Persist!' as if cheering a pole-vaulter to leap higher into the air. This is a word that was spoken frequently during our conversations this summer in Ireland and in England. I persisted. He resisted. That resistance was with a certain wryness. He seems professorial, with his thickly tufted hair and eyebrows and his quietly assured manner of speaking. In portraits and photographs, his chin is often resting on his hand as he regards the world with a slyness: the thinker about to spring into a witticism.

During our meetings, the time he was most relaxed was at a long and convivial dinner in Dublin with his producer, Noel Pearson; his wife, Anne Friel, and their youngest daughter, Judy, who is a theatre director. With no tape recorder or notepad in sight – and with everyone drinking a fine Bordeaux – he became expansive, even disagreeing with his wife over one of his favourite subjects, the efficacy of presenting English adaptations of foreign classics in Ireland. He insisted the language should be adapted into Irish-English. Anne Friel, quite correctly I think, suggested it might be possible to write a neutral translation that would work for all English-speaking countries. 'A neutered translation!' Friel countered, and broke into an impassioned defence of his nationalistic position.

One of Friel's favourite recent novels is *Amongst Women*, by John McGahern. His own life story could also bear that title, for he has spent his years amongst women, beginning with his Glenties aunts. Actually there were seven sisters, but he reduced them to five in the play ('Economy is more important than truth,' he says with a smile). He has two sisters, one living in Ireland, one in England, and he and his wife have four daughters and one son.

During his boyhood near Omagh in County Tyrone and later in

Derry, his mother was a dominant, vivacious presence. Friel's father was a teacher and school principal, remembered by his son as a quiet, reserved man. On each side of the family, one grand-parent was illiterate, a fact that reminds Friel of his peasant roots. One sign of the closeness of the two families is that Friel's father was best man at the wedding of Anne Friel's parents. Brian and Anne Friel, married for thirty-seven years, have known each other since they were sixteen.

Friel was born, grew up and still lives within an area of sixty miles. For someone who has resolutely stayed at home, it is inter-esting that he so often writes about questions of exile and emigra-tion, as in *Philadelphia, Here I Come!*, the play that brought him an international reputation at the age of thirty-five.

When asked why he himself has remained homebound, Friel replied: 'I think exile can be acquired sitting in the same place for the rest of your life. Physical exile is not necessary.' In his mind, Friel has gone to Philadelphia and farther, questioning his sense of dislocation and reflecting in himself his country's own unsure identity. But by remaining in his own corner of Ireland, he has found his constantly replenished source of inspiration.

He did not set out to be a writer. He went to St Patrick's College in Maynooth with the idea of studying for the priesthood, but at the age of seventeen, he changed his mind. When asked if he could imagine himself as a priest, he answered, 'It would somehow have been in conflict with my belief in paganism.' Instead he followed his father and his sisters into the teaching profession. Gradually he began to divert more of his attention to writing short stories, which soon began appearing regularly in *The New Yorker*. Stories led to radio plays and then to stage plays; his first was presented in Belfast in 1959.

He might have continued quietly on his modest career were it not for Tyrone Guthrie. The legendary stage director, who lived in County Monaghan, sent Friel a fan letter about one of the *New Yorker* stories. They met, and this led to a firm friendship. Guthrie was about to go to America to inaugurate the Tyrone Guthrie Theatre in Minneapolis. Friel went with him as an unpaid observer. The months he spent watching Guthrie would prove to be among the most important in his life. Sitting by his side as

Guthrie staged *Hamlet*, *The Miser*, *Three Sisters* and other plays, with Hume Cronyn, Jessica Tandy and George Grizzard, Friel was fully immersed in the theatre art, its practice as well as its theories.

Searching for a way to describe Guthrie's importance to him, he said, 'The experience was enabling to the extent that it gave me courage and daring to attempt things.' When Friel's money ran thin, he returned to Ireland, where he wrote *Philadelphia, Here I Come!*, a stunning departure in style and artistic authority.

Over the next dozen years, he wrote almost a play a year. Although many of them came to New York, he remained more of a figure in his home country than in England or the USA. Then came a breakthrough. In a period of about eighteen months, beginning in 1979, he wrote three of his best plays, *Aristocrats*, *Faith Healer* and *Translations*.

Faith Healer, an eloquent metaphorical study of the artist's life and death struggle, had a very brief life on Broadway through a combination of unfortuitous circumstances. A play of four seemingly contradictory monologues, it did not sit comfortably on a large Broadway stage. But even in New York it had its ardent admirers. After the final performance, James Mason, who played the title role, addressed the audience. As he began speaking about 'the Broadway failure' of the play, theatre-goers shouted in protest, 'No. Never. Never.' Subsequent productions have reclaimed *Faith Healer*, at the centre of Friel's canon, as his most personal statement about art and faith. At a climactic moment in the play, the faith healer, Frank Hardy, accepts his fate and faces his assassins: 'And as I moved across that yard towards them and offered myself to them, then for the first time I had a simple and genuine sense of home-coming. Then for the first time there was no atrophying terror; and the maddening questions were silent. At long last I was renouncing chance.'

It was to be ten years before *Aristocrats*, his most Chekhovian play, came to the USA, opening at the Manhattan Theatre Club, which also produced *Translations*. These two plays reaffirmed the artistry evidenced years before in *Philadelphia*. But the ready acceptance of *Translations* in England prompted the author to an act of self-subversion. He wrote a farce spoofing issues raised in the earlier work. The play, *The Communication Cord*, was not well received.

What followed was a period of silence and frustration. Despite his apparent productivity, there had been fallow times in the past, but none like the middle 1980s. Ostensibly he was working on an historical play about the Irish hero Hugh O'Neill. Every morning he would go up to his study in his house in Greencastle in County Donegal. That house, a converted temperance hotel, is only a few steps from the sea, the Lough Foyle. He would sit at his desk, with a cigarette in his hand and with his back to the vista. As usual, he wrote in pencil. The play proceeded at a crawl. Looking back on the long bleak period, he said: 'I sat it out. I waited for the rescue.' One could imagine him saying to himself: 'Persist! Persist!'

Encouraged by his wife to find a divergence, he wrote an adaptation of Turgenev's *Fathers and Sons*. At the end of that labour he journeyed to London and listened to Tom Kilroy's suggestions for writing a play about his aunts. Shortly thereafter, he was buoyed by the delayed opening and success of *Aristocrats* in New York. As he began to write *Dancing at Lughnasa*, he focused the play on the sisters and the home-coming of their brother, a burned-out priest who has served for many years as a missionary in Africa. Although he had written a number of plays with women as central characters, this was the first time he was able to deal so directly with his mother and her family.

Over the years, Friel has become increasingly mobile, flying from Derry to Dublin to London, but the longer he is away from Donegal, the more unsettled he feels. For all his talk of exile-at-home, he is rock-rooted and as indigenous as his art. His home is his refuge. There he is surrounded by familiarity – his books, his collections of Irish paintings and antique clocks, his beehives and the natural beauty of the landscape. Only seventy-five miles away he has a summer house facing the Atlantic.

Now that the Friel children are grown, with each involved in a profession (the oldest daughter has the euphonious job of being a curator in a castle in Kilkenny; their son recently completed his studies in marine biology), the house is quiet, except at holiday time. Friends from other parts of Ireland, and occasionally America, stop by, and Friel is quick to play the host. One of his most welcome guests is Katharine Hepburn.

His circle of intimates is literary as well as theatrical, beginning with Seamus Heaney, Ireland's premier poet, with whom he shares both background and artistic sensibility. Heaney and other friends are involved in Field Day, the company that Friel and the actor Stephen Rea founded to tour plays and generate a nation-wide, politically conscious theatre.

Anne Friel is the first to read her husband's plays, although, she says, he has the annoying habit of giving her a play when it is only half-finished, leaving her to surmise where it might end. For her, her husband has something of a split personality, combining the utmost seriousness with great humour. He is, she says, like the doubled character, the private and public man, in *Philadelphia, Here I Come!*.

During one of our talks, referring to the fact that he no longer wrote short stories, I began, 'Having moved from fiction to thea-tre . . .' He interrupted, 'Theatre is fiction, too.' He explained that the characters in *Dancing at Lughnasa* diverged from precise real-ity. Speaking of the women of Glenties, he said, 'The play pro-vides me with an acceptable fiction for them now.'

In his introduction to his adaptation of *The London Vertigo*, an eighteenth-century comedy by Charles Macklin, Friel says, 'The desire to metamorphose oneself, to change everything utterly – name, beliefs, voice, loyalties, language, ambitions, even one's appearance – secretly excites most people at some stage of their lives.'[1] The statement seemed curious, coming from one who has remained so firmly in place. But as a playwright, he said, he meta-morphoses himself through his work. 'You invent an alternative life, a fiction of your life each time you write a play.'

To the suggestion that there still might be a real alternative life he would like to lead, he said, with enthusiasm: 'I would love to be a very good clarinettist, or trumpeter or organist. But those are pipedream alternatives.' He continued: 'Had I been born fifty years earlier, exile would have certainly been valuable, maybe even nec-essary. There was no encouragement for artists in those years.'

'The question', he said, 'is not whether Ireland is harder or eas-ier on its artists. The artist has to acquire his own armour and armoury. I don't have a lot of sympathy with people who feel they are silenced by opposition.' In his career, he has deliberately moved from theatre to theatre, from director to director, taking the widest advantage of Ireland's relatively small pool of theatri-cal talent. If he worked with the same people each time, he said, he 'would acquire a dependence, a comfort, a house style'. He adds: 'You could absorb the style of a director. It's necessary to maintain your freedom, your individuality.'

Despite his feelings about Guthrie and several directors with whom he has worked, he has grave doubts about the directorial profession. 'I want a director to call rehearsals, to make sure the actors are there on time and to get them to speak their lines clearly and distinctly,' he says. 'I've no interest whatever in his concept or interpretation. I think it's almost a bogus career. When did these people appear on the scene? One hundred years ago?' And he added, 'I think we can dispose of them very easily again.' By his measure a director should be 'obedient' to the play. If not, all you need is an 'efficient stage manager'.

He makes his revisions before a play goes into rehearsal. 'As far as I'm concerned, there is a final and complete orchestra score. All I want is musicians to play it. I'm not going to rewrite the second movement for the sake of the oboe player.' Then he admitted: 'I sound very dogmatic and grossly self-assured about this, but I don't feel that way at all. I just think it is a more valuable stance than working on the hoof. For the actor, the score is there and there are musical notations all around. We call them stage directions.' For example, the Dionysiac dance in *Lughnasa* is carefully choreographed in the text itself.

To safeguard his work, he attends all rehearsals of a new play. But once the play has opened, he leaves it, and it is with the greatest reluctance that he will look at a second production. Part of that clearly derives from his proximity to his art. To illustrate, he told a story about Ibsen. He said that when Ibsen returned to Norway towards the end of his life, he was given permission to sit in the royal garden. 'Every day Ibsen would strut along, this pompous little figure in his frock-coat and tall hat.' He would sit on a bench, take off his hat and put it on his knee. 'Someone realized he was staring into his hat and crept up behind him and saw that inside the crown of the hat was a mirror. And this is how Ibsen spent his day.

'Whether or not that story is true, that is the kind of narcissism writers have. If one takes art as seriously as the faith healer does, as a matter of life and death, that itself is hubristic. You're courting catastrophe.' Knowing that, he still persists. 'As Auden said, art is not going to save the Jews from the Holocaust. It's not going to make a person any more worthy or noble, but I do think it can make some tiny, thumbscrew adjustment on our psyche.'

Friel writes only what he wants to write – plays, not screenplays – and refuses to repeat himself. 'If *Dancing at Lughnasa* is about the necessity for paganism', he said, then his next play [*Wonderful Tennessee*] will deal with 'the necessity for mystery. It's mystery, not religion, but mystery finds its expression in this society mostly in religious practice.' The working title is *The Imagined Place*.

In one of his early stories, he wrote about a father who reluctantly goes with his wife and children to revisit his birthplace in Donegal and discovers 'the ruins of the old place'. At first, the father reflects that the past is 'a mirage – a soft illusion into which one steps in order to escape the present.' But by the end of the story, he has come to terms with his memories. 'The past did have meaning,' he realizes. 'It was neither reality nor dreams . . . It was simply continuance, life repeating itself and surviving.'

Dancing at Lughnasa arrives on Broadway in the Abbey Theatre production, directed by Patrick Mason and starring the Irish actresses who created the roles or played them at London's National Theatre, including Rosaleen Linehan as the oldest sister and Catherine Byrne as the youngest, representing Friel's mother. Joining the company as the missionary is Donal Donnelly. For the actor, the play is itself a home-coming. He has had a long history in the works of Friel, appearing on Broadway in *Philadelphia, Here I Come!* and *Faith Healer*.

Before coming to New York, *Dancing at Lughnasa* gave one special performance in Glenties, the market town in the hills of Donegal that was the setting of the original events in the play. The occasion was a Brian Friel festival, a week-long series of talks, panel discussions and performances sponsored by the Patrick MacGill Summer School. For weeks before the festival, Friel tormented himself with the question of whether or not he should attend. Although he felt close to many of the people who would participate, the idea made him feel acutely self-conscious. Finally he decided to go, but to avoid all colloquies analysing Frielian themes, like immigration and return, incipient decay and the illusion of pastoralism, and certainly to avoid the guided bus tour of 'Friel country'. Still, he felt 'like a ghost at the feast'.

The festival opened on a Sunday night in August with the performance of *Dancing at Lughnasa* at the Glenties Comprehensive School with actors gathered from the Abbey company and the current London cast. The lighting and sound equipment came from Dublin, the costumes had been delayed in transit from London and the scenery was makeshift. To give a semblance of reality, several haystacks were brought indoors to stand in for the wheat field in the original production. Every seat in the school hall was taken.

Overcoming his embarrassment at all the attention, Friel addressed the audience before the performance. He said it was 'an important occasion' for him because the play had to do with his family, which had lived a half mile from the school hall. In the audience were many neighbours who knew the people behind the characters. After thanking the actors, the playwright stood to one side of the house to watch the brave Glenties women take the stage. The performance began late and was not finished until after midnight, when the audience rose in a wave and cheered. For Friel, it was 'a heightened and very moving' experience. Art and life had come together in the real Ballybeg.

Preface to *A Month in the Country* (1992)

Turgenev called *A Month in the Country* a comedy, just as Chekhov called *The Cherry Orchard* and *The Seagull* comedies. They were not formally categorizing these plays, I believe, but wished to indicate their own amused and ironic attitude to their characters and the situations those characters found themselves in. But I think that to call *A Month in the Country* a comedy today is restricting to the play: it imposes a reading on the text and suggests a response to it that could be inhibiting to actors and audience. *A Month in the Country* is certainly not a tragedy. Neither is it a comedy. Perhaps we should settle for 'a play in five scenes'.

I have attributed to the characters the ages given in T. A. Greenan's standard text. But I think that all of those parts could and perhaps should be played by slightly older actors. And I trust I will not offend the purists by tinkering with the Russian names and forms of address.

A literal translation of Turgenev's text was done for me by Christopher Heaney. From it I have composed this very free version. In places it may not be reverent to the original but nowhere, I hope, is it unfaithful to its spirit.

Ivan Turgenev (1818–1883)

Two years before his death, on one of his compulsive return visits to Russia, Turgenev stopped off at St Petersburg to visit Tolstoy and Sonya at Yasnaya Polyana. The date was 22 August 1881. It was Sonya's birthday. The house was full of guests. Turgenev was then a celebrated writer with a huge – Tolstoy thought inflated – reputation. To the young guests at the party, most of whom had never been beyond Petersburg, he was mesmerizing, an exotic: well over six feet, handsome, charming, a bachelor, magnificently dressed, multilingual, in this gathering flamboyantly, even aggressively, European; and of course internationally famous. They questioned him about his work, about London, about literary trends, about his Oxford degree. Their hunger and their awe lured him into garrulity and exaggeration. Avoiding Tolstoy's cold eye he launched into witty stories about the latest fashions in Paris. And then suddenly the sixty-three-year-old writer jumped to his feet, threw off his gold jacket, stuck his thumbs into his silk waistcoat and gave an exuberant demonstration of the dance that was all the rage on the French vaudeville stage – the cancan. After a few minutes, breathless and exhausted, he collapsed into an armchair.

That night in his diary Tolstoy, younger than Turgenev by ten years but more knowing by a score, commemorated the event – not his wife's birthday but Turgenev's exhibition. He wrote, 'August 22. Turgenev. Sad.'

The entry was tart but off-centre. Turgenev was not sad. He was confused. All his days he was a ditherer, racked between irreconcilable beliefs and compulsions. An instinctive revolutionary who needed the complacency of conservatism. A Slavophile whose heart loved Russia with an intuitive passion but who offered his mind to Europe to mould. A writer who was never sure whether he was a dramatist, a novelist, a poet or an essayist. A bachelor who throughout his entire life loved the married Pauline Viardot faithfully and without reservation – but who fathered a child by a servant-girl and had several casual affairs with discreet women. A dramatist who believed his plays should be read, not performed, and who could not make up his mind whether to call this play *The Student* or *Two Women* or *A Month in the Country*. A sportsman who enjoyed grouse-shooting in Scotland and painting in the south of France but who was always haunted by a sense that real life, a life of content and fulfilment, had somehow eluded him but was available elsewhere, if only he could locate just where.

But for all his vacillations, the inner man, the assured artist, was organized and practical. With what Graham Greene once called 'admirable domestic economy' he marshalled all these irreconcilables and put them to use in his work. Vacillation, the inability to act decisively, the longing to be other, to be elsewhere, became the very core of his dramatic action. He fashioned a new kind of dramatic situation and a new kind of dramatic character where for the first time psychological and poetic elements create a theatre of moods and where the action resides in internal emotion and secret turmoil and not in external events. We now have a name for that kind of drama: we call it Chekhovian. But in *A Month in the Country* Turgenev had written Chekhovian characters and situations forty-six years before Chekhov wrote his first fully Chekhovian play, *The Seagull*.

A Month in the Country was first performed at the Maly Theatre in 1872, more than twenty years after it was completed. The newness of its form baffled audiences and critics. Because it eluded classification they called it 'old-fashioned' and 'undramatic'. Turgenev had to wait a further seven years for a new production and a warmer reception. Then came Chekhov a decade later; and the new form was crafted to shimmering perfection. The undramatic became the new drama. And in the years to follow, *A Month in the Country* found acceptance in the slipstream of Chekhov's astonishing achievement.

The term metabiosis in chemistry denotes a mode of living in which one organism is dependent on another for the preparation of an environment in which it can live. The relationship between Turgenev and Chekhov was richly metabiotic. *A Month in the Country* was before its time and moved haltingly across unmapped territory. But it established the necessary environment in which Chekhov could blossom. And once Chekhov had achieved his full stature, once Chekhovian drama was confidently established, the environment was again ready for the reclamation and reassessment and full understanding of Turgenev's pioneering work. So they gave life to each other. And between them they changed the face of European drama.

Extracts from a Sporadic Diary
(1992–94): *Molly Sweeney*

28 August 1992

Went to an eye specialist in Letterkenny yesterday. He says I have incipient cataracts (just the aging process?) and perhaps glaucoma. He is to arrange a meeting with an ophthalmologist in Altnagelvin Hospital in Derry.

29 August 1992

The examination is set up – 10 a.m. in Altnagelvin next Monday. A young ophthalmologist with a good reputation.

10 November 1992

Still looking for something to fill the gap left by the completion of WONDERFUL TENNESSEE. I might look at an adaptation. Gogol, maybe? THE INSPECTOR GENERAL?[1] Why does THE LADY WITH THE DOG keep coming back to me?

12 November 1992

Doing nothing. A sense of emptiness. Too lethargic even to do this. Reading.

15 December 1992

Not working. Not even circling around anything. Reading fitfully and indiscriminately.

1 January 1993

A passing reference in a biography of Dostoievsky that Turgenev and Dostoievsky both took part in a production of Gogol's THE

INSPECTOR GENERAL. Interesting – however unlikely. Who is the Irish Turgenev?

2 January 1993

Dostoievsky – anti-Semitic, anti-Protestant, anti-Catholic: 'You judge very rightly when you opine that I hold all evil to be grounded in disbelief, and maintain that he who abjures nationalism abjures faith also . . . A Russian who abjures nationalism is either an atheist or indifferent to religious questions . . .'

4 January 1993

Four empty months stretch ahead until WONDERFUL TENNESSEE rehearsals. I feel I ought to have something in hand, planned. Another translation? A dramatized life of Dostoievsky? Something to do with Turgenev and Dostoievsky, those rivals and diametrically opposite [writers], together doing Gogol's THE INSPECTOR GENERAL – with Gogol in the cast?

20 January 1993

Why is it that the (very badly translated) letters of Bulgakov and the diaries of his wife seemed vivid and irresistible in 1937 when the trials and the purges were at their most indiscriminate? Around that time Bulgakov wrote a play about Stalin (when Mandelstam was in prison – Akhmatova in despair – Pasternak, Prokofiev, Shostakovich all in deep trouble). Why does a life touch us at the point when it abandons the Great Virtues and scurries around in frantic despair? (The wife's letters/diaries with their distancing comments on their friends who have been arrested, [and] have disappeared: 'Nemesis has been visited on . . .' 'I always detested that man . . .') Why do we then join in the official chorus? Self-protection only? But [do] we *believe* what we say? Why is cowardice at the centre of our lives? Bulgakov wrote to Stalin (as Mandelstam did) again and again. And to Gorky, Gorky the hero, who had 'access'. And did Gorky himself believe?

26 January 1993

C. G. Jung: 'It is important to have a secret, a premonition of

things unknown. It fills life with something impersonal, a numi-
nosum. A man who has never experienced that has missed something important. He must sense that he lives in a world which in
some respects is mysterious; that things happen and can be experienced which remain inexplicable; that not everything that happens
can be anticipated. The unexpected and the incredible belong in
this world. Only then is life whole. For me the world has from the
beginning been infinite and ungraspable.' WONDERFUL TENNESSEE?

14 March 1993

Not working. Nothing simmering. The mad hope that miraculously a fully-formed play will leap from the head. And why not?

15 July 1993

First stirrings of a possible play. A man/woman loses sight at five
years of age. Blind for thirty-five years. Sight (partially) restored.
  Have ordered various books and papers on this subject.

27 July 1993

Wondering sporadically about the sight play. Vaporous notions
that appear and disappear occasionally.
  I tell myself that I am waiting for the reading material and *then*
the play will manifest itself with dizzying luminosity!

29 July 1993

> 'I do not know which to prefer,
> The beauty of inflections
> Or the beauty of innuendoes,
> The blackbird whistling
> Or just after.'[2]

  The sight-blind play?

30 July 1993

Sniffing around – more focused than sniffing – the blind-sight
idea. (I lose interest and then come across a phrase like 'mentally
blind' or 'agnosic' or 'blind-sight' – and the barb sinks into the

side of the mouth.[3] Or a word like 'gnosis', i.e. long periods of impaired vision, blurriness, which reaches out to gnosis, a knowledge of mystical things.)

And aware, too – indeed uneasy – that too much sniffing can induce addiction; a point of no return; a commitment to a journey that hasn't earned – doesn't inspire – belief.

Cave [beware!]. (But sniff on!)

1 August 1993

Maybe: a blind person functioning perfectly well in a familiar situation; the promise of sight; operation; consequences. If sight restored is used as a metaphor then it will be blunt and crude. But why not *document* – without extension, without hint of analogue – the story of a blind person? A medical story that is also offered as a love/spiritual story?

7 August 1993

The play seems to be gathering round three people. Is the blind person a man or woman? My *instinct* at this stage is a woman.

8 August 1993

Is it time to sit down at the blind play?

9 August 1993

The answer to the question above is No. But it is necessary to be *attentive* to it. Later – courtship.

12 August 1993

Making notes on the blind play. Constantly being diverted from the central issue which is: Who are these people and what is their story? – not How is their story told?

> 'She says, "I am content when wakened birds,
> Before they fly, test the reality
> Of misty fields, by their sweet questionings;
> But when the birds are gone, and their warm fields
> Return no more, where, then, is paradise?"'[4]

Blackbirds – wakened birds – innuendoes – testing reality – sight restored?

13 August 1993

Every day adding a few lines to the notes on the blind play. Today I think the play is about seeking – and fabricating – paradise. (The result of reading W. S.'s poetry?)

24 August 1993

I have got a lot of blind material from my agent and have been reading it closely – Valvo, Strampelli, Berkeley, Locke, Van Sinden, Sacks, etc. etc.

No idea at all if there is a vein there.

25 August 1993

Working through the blind books with diminishing relish. My instinct is to toss them aside and confront the play directly.

31 August 1993

Weary of reading about prostheses, nystagmus, visual and tactile experience, etc. etc. Back to fundamentals:
a person is restored to sight
the experience is enormously difficult
the new world is a disappointment – the old world was better
the person goes into a decline and dies

15 September 1993

Time to look again at the blind play. I haven't worked at the material for some time but I have a sense that it is stirring in the background. And the shape it seems to be claiming is a three-hander – a woman, two men. Maybe not distinct monologues; contrapuntal; overlapping.

22 September 1993

There are three voices – in fact the play is a trio for three voices: the blind/cured wife, her husband, the ophthalmologist.

The men force her to be sighted. The process kills her.

8 November 1993

If/when I go back to the blind play I must approach it more easily, more openly, not schematically. Allow it to flow easily through me. Don't try to control the erratic transiliences.

> You are the music
> While the music lasts.

Where in Eliot?[5]
Freud: 'The final therapy is work and love.'

9 November 1993

The desk is cleared. The blind books are arrayed before me. The play is chronologically due – but maybe not spiritually? An innate sense of duty, the work ethic, years of discipline – all conspire to force a beginning. And why not?

22 November 1993

The blind play keeps getting snagged in complex medical explanations. The various eye books keep demanding attention. But the play is about *people* and the medical condition of one of these people mustn't be allowed to dominate.

23 November 1993

The play – the play – the play! *Of course* it won't begin to stir until I know everything about these people – first.

24 November 1993

Turgenev wrote A MONTH IN THE COUNTRY in 1850. It was first successfully produced in 1879 (with Maria Savina). He doesn't seem to have cared; was astonished at the success then. The more I read about him the more convinced I am that he was an *amateur*. What attracted him was the *idea* of being a writer, a painter, a traveller, a linguist, a European, *a Russian exile*. And who loves Russia more than a Russian exile?

The idea of a metabiotic relationship between himself and Chekhov should be looked at. Turgenev's (failed) play created an atmosphere sympathetic to Chekhov's new drama. And the success of that new drama made possible the warm revival of Turgenev.

29 November 1993

The blind play is stationary; hasn't even the first stirrings of movement. I think because I don't know anything about Martha (?) apart from her condition. Is she even a woman?

30 November 1993

I have a sense that if I begin to put them (the characters) down on paper they will become – gradually – corporeal. It's a method, I suppose.

1 December 1993

A letter from the ophthalmologist in Altnagelvin Hospital: I am to have the eye operation there next Monday. I'll be in the hospital, I'm told, from 10 a.m. until 4 p.m. Or I may stay in overnight.

2 December 1993

The blind play is trammelled by basic questions. The characters (how many?) are acquiring some definition – not a lot. But their *method* of revealing themselves is nowhere near a solution. (And although I write that, I keep casting the play in monologues; or duets; or trios; but not in any kind of usual dramatic exchange.)

8 December 1993

Altnagelvin at 10 a.m. on Monday. Operation on the right eye – 1.15 p.m. to 2 p.m.
  Left the hospital at 3.45 p.m.
  Back yesterday to get the bandages off. 'Perfect!' said the ophthalmologist.
  Due back next Monday.
  Have written two longish first monologues – husband and wife. But looking at them both today I know that both are wrong –

wrong in pitch and in tone but more importantly wrong in form.

9 December 1993

Since I've had the operation on the right eye this ink is quintessential blackness, the page blinding white. The new eye hasn't learned to discriminate – it is equally impressed by everything. So that reality has a sur-reality that alters, adjusts, distorts everything. But no more pain.

11 December 1993

The eye improves daily. Occasionally a sense that there is an eyelash in it. Or that a tiny, circular haze tags along just behind the line of vision. But the sight is immeasurably better. Now the left eye seems useless.

12 December 1993

The blind play is going nowhere. Nowhere near lift-off.
  Getting irritable – worse, *weary* – with it all.

13 December 1993

Over the weekend I wrote the wife's first speech. A dozen times. And again this morning.
  I'm not unhappy with it. The sound is real enough. The tone is right enough. A woman may materialize.
  If I could get the ophthalmologist's first speech today . . .

14 December 1993

Called back to Altnagelvin for a check-up this morning. All's well.
  The wife's first speech doesn't seem so accomplished today.

14 [*sic*] December 1993

Got an opening statement from the ophthalmologist. Nowhere near an individual voice; but a kind of Identikit picture of the man emerging.
  Wrote the statement a second time. Now even the Identikit is gone.

18 December 1993

Attempting to move on to the husband's voice. Have got something on paper for the wife and ophthalmologist. Faltering. But at least marks on paper.

20 December 1993

I now have something down for all three and each piece instantly demands adjustments in the previous piece. So everything is fluid. And as I write each character it is clear that they can't be *written* but can only evolve, developing (and revealing) their characters and characteristics as they discover themselves, not as I add to them, compose them.

21 December 1993

On one of his trips back to Russia Turgenev, the sixty-year-old, fully Europeanized, foppishly dressed, altogether elegant artist, had dinner with Tolstoy and his family. They persuaded (maliciously?) Turgenev to demonstrate the latest dance craze – the cancan. Turgenev in his vanity did. And in his diary that night Tolstoy wrote: 'Turgenev. Cancan. Sad.'

22 December 1993

Something wrong with the ophthalmologist. I'm not getting him. The elements are all there but they don't cohere. I've written his first speech eight times, I'm sure.

26 December 1993

Synge's intro. to PLAYBOY: '. . . Ibsen and Zola dealing with the reality of life in joyless and pallid words. On the stage one must have reality, and one must have joy . . . In a good play every speech should be as fully flavoured as a nut or apple . . .'

27 December 1993

Every day over the Christmas period I sat at the desk and read the first three speeches. They *are* the voices of three distinct people. And I think they are pitched right. (Of course they'll be rewritten a dozen more times.) But I'm not sure of two things: are they speaking at the appropriate time in their lives; and is this – now – the right time to feed the information. (So much of this is arbitrary. Timing is less important – at this stage – than tone.)

30 December 1993

Various interruptions. Comings and goings. Discomfort (at least) with the right eye. But every day obeisance has been made to the manuscript.

It is without joy. But what is there is there, waiting to be added to. And doing this entry is both a gesture to the discipline and an act of evasion. Because just now I'm writing this to avoid the big hurdle of Martha's second monologue.

7 January 1994

The new play – form, theme, characters – is *so* like FAITH HEALER. A second candlestick on the mantelpiece; a second china dog.

17 January 1994

The play stutters on, the Overall retreating further and further and each tiny section taking on a bloated and distorting importance.

I go back to Altnagelvin hospital tomorrow. I'm very uneasy with the new eye. I don't seem able to accommodate it. It flaunts its power.

23 January 1994

First act completed (sort of). Didn't go near the desk yesterday.

Anne thinks it is too short. Maybe.

What is lost, so far, is the overreaching, perhaps excessive, notion that this could be a trio – all three voices speaking simultaneously, in immediate sequence, in counterpoint, in harmony, in discord. Instead I have a simple linear narrative in traditional form; with the language, sentiments and modest ambitions of FAITH HEALER – without FAITH HEALER's austerity.

Act 2 must be post-operation – with excursions back and forward.

24 January 1994

Should Act 1 be longer? Perhaps yes. Perhaps a Martha–Frank courtship sequence, then a Martha–Frank marriage sequence? They could be valuable as long as they are pre-operation.

25 January 1994

The play is at a standstill. Because Anne said Act 1 was too short?

26 January 1994

Difficulty: to balance the material in such a way that the medical element is essential but always subservient to the human. This means that the medical-technical processes and language have to be so thoroughly absorbed that all that is left is the watermark, the coloration.

Today just sitting at the desk . . . being available. It is probably more accurate to say that the author haunts the theme than to say that the theme haunts the author.

28 January 1994

Act 1 finished – again. All I can say is that it is longer.

31 January 1994

Act 1 has its shape. I have a lot of work to do on it but I'm not unhappy with it.

The unease now is that Act 2 could easily and very rapidly sink into a long whinge. To delicately draw the arc that carries us from the 'successful' operation, through disenchantment, to giving up.

1 February 1994

The right eye is bullying me. I think I'm sorry I had the operation. I will have to go back to the ophthalmologist. Wrestling with various kinds of glasses – driving, reading, TV.

8 February 1994

First two monologues (Martha, Frank) of Act 2 done. Now stuck (hence this) at Rice. I'm stuck with him because I don't know his story, I think.

Titles: MARTHA. VISIONS.

14 February 1994

Back at the desk, trying to plug into the rhythms of the play. Still stuck with Rice.

Title: VISION.

17 February 1994

Still haven't got Rice's monologue but something *is* on paper and I should get it. Part of the difficulty now is to keep firm control of the flow of 'facts' and 'information' on that whole rich period between Bandages Off and Despair – all that delight, all that terror for all of them – to reveal the complete range *and* the emotional transition.

24 February 1994

Into the final stretch of the play: a sequence (or two? or three?) of very short monologues, followed by three long, concluding (and difficult – no, tricky) monologues. Then start at the beginning again.

14 March 1994

Last night I wrote the final paragraph of the final monologue (Molly's). Her name and the title of the play changed once more – now MOLLY SWEENEY.

28 March 1994

Now, this morning, after two weeks' absence, back to MOLLY SWEENEY.

3 April 1994, Easter Sunday

Finished MOLLY SWEENEY on Good Friday, 1 April. Now I'm retyping – and reworking – it in a kind of fury.

6 April 1994

The play, MOLLY SWEENEY, goes to the typist this evening. The only emotion on having finished it is relief: to emerge, blinking, into the sunlight.

Extracts from a Sporadic Diary:
Give Me Your Answer, Do! (1995–96)[1]

4 March 1995

Hanging on desperately to the one, wan, casual, insubstantial, unwilling idea. An artist – in a wheelchair? – a birthday (sixtieth?) party? His wife. Their – his – friends. And the phantom thought that the Husband/Artist and Wife employ a duologue that (a) moves on totally different levels so that there is no *apparent* exchange between them; (b) consists every so often of interior monologue that sounds as if it were a *normal* part of their duologue but is in fact emerging from a private depth. (This could be accomplished technically by using a distinctive vocal tone.) Because in life every duologue is composed of the spoken and the unspoken. (When the unspoken is spoken, it is as if the actor puts on a vocal mask.)

4 April 1995

Panic sets in when nothing stirs, when even the wish to sit at the desk has gone. A conviction that it is finally over. And of course that condition *will* come. And why not now?

I look at the row of Wittgenstein books on the shelf. Nothing. In the past I had notebooks, etc. etc. Now – nothing.

15 April 1995, Easter Saturday

Not working – worse still, the prospect of not working – becomes a kind of malaise that is on the verge of becoming a breakdown. And trying to decide whether (a) to sit it out; (b) face it out; (c) just write – anything; all becomes part of the acute distress. Indeed the act of writing this is an attempt to postpone total atrophy.

And shouldn't this be a day close to resurrection?

16 April 1995

If you just sit and wait – deliberately alert and open – keeping despair and anger at bay – trying not to worry about spent mines and dried wells – will It happen? Why should it?

17 April 1995

Dipping the toe into Wittgenstein again. Especially his belief that the job of the philosopher is to represent the relationship between language and the world. (a) Philosophy cannot answer its traditional questions in meaningful language, i.e. descriptive, scientific language. (b) In imposing the self-discipline of *saying only what can be said* and thus enjoining silence in the realm of metaphysics, genuine metaphysical impulses are released. The unsayable is not said but it is nevertheless manifest. The very act of taking care to say only what can be said 'shows' another silent realm beyond language (and logic) and so beyond description. And what is beyond description, what is trivialized by the doomed attempt to describe, is what is important in human life . . . [2]

Who said – Engelmann? – that the job of the philosopher is like the job of the cartographer who maps the coastline of an island – not to learn the boundaries of the island but to learn the limits of the ocean?

Much help from J. H. in all this (WITTGENSTEIN).

8 June 1995

Kitezh in Russian folklore is a city that vanishes from sight when marauders approach. As it disappears its bell keeps ringing through the fog.

Rimsky-Korsakov opera (?). Akhmatova poem, 'The Way of all Earth'.[3]

12 June 1995

Went to Monaghan to pick up a (small) swarm of bees from T. B. J O'H came over and helped me to put them into the hive. The swarm so small that J O'H says it's touch and go if they'll survive. And there are only four brood frames intact in the chamber – moths had eaten huge holes in the comb. I put in three damaged sections to feed the new swarm.

Looked at them later. Flying. Quite active.

Today, as a tentative act of commitment, will start making notes on the artist/his papers idea. The trouble is that by doing that, that tentative step is irrevocable (can one revoke a step?) and I am almost certainly committing myself to something I know nothing about. Frightening.

Began. The A4 pages cut in half. The treasury tag. The capital A in red ink on the front page.

24 June 1995

Eight days of short notes. Small areas – altogether peripheral to the core of the play, whatever *that* might be – are beginning to find shape. But the spring, the engine, the drive is missing.

29 June 1995

More and more notes. I suppose that means that there will soon be no retreat.

3 July 1995

Nothing done since.

A very strange and very vivid dream last night. Have just bought a very large decayed house. I am being shown round it. Suddenly a small creature – a mouse? – races towards me at great speed and launches itself at me. I kick it accurately. It goes into the air and lands at the feet of a maid. It is an exquisitely coloured, strange bird. Slightly dazed but fine. The maid says, 'It's a cross old thing. Don't worry. It'll be fine.' She walks away. The bird walks – waddles – after her.

The dream has echoes of another dream that recurs. A very large house on top of a hill, at the end of a long straight avenue. The details of this dream vary. But a constant is that the house is occupied by something, somebody (female, I think) of unspeakable evil and indescribable ugliness.

And the play?

13 July 1995

Couldn't sit down today. The play is retreating. What play?

28 July 1995

Persistent unease with having the writer/artist as the central character. Maybe if that key issue were resolved – either submit to the idea or give him a different trade – maybe the play would move.

1 August 1995

I suppose – no, I know – that the question has to be faced: do I scrap whatever remnants of a theme there are lying about – those tatty, tawdry bits of ideas; put them out of my mind? Or do I persist with what I have and hope to nurture it into something worthwhile?

The question has to be faced. NOW.

And of course it won't be faced. The dallying, the vacillation, the messing can go on for weeks, months.

Lughnasa time.

4 August 1995

Pursuing this play (play?) is like opening a matrioska: each replica that emerges is of a progressively diminishing size.

16 August 1995

The bees are very busy. The heatwave, I suppose. I didn't intend putting in a super this year because the season is far on. But I did today. We'll see. At least it will give the bees more room.

The notes are scattered around me. The writer is dead? – alive? That still unresolved. I've also thought of the writer dead but appearing to his wife only.

2 September 1995

On the radio this a.m. (*Talkback*) heard a letter written in the 1880s by a woman who had emigrated from Ireland to Australia. Beautifully poised, delicately phrased, *deeply* moving. Its authenticity was luminous. And its freshness and truth made me wonder: What mean, introverted, narrow, narcissistic people – especially the writer – am I dealing with in this play? And suddenly I didn't hate them – I had no interest in them.

(The woman in Australia enclosed £3 'to buy a drink'. 'And does the water still pour into the yard?')

169

28 January 1996

When am I going to look again at the writer/selling-his-papers play? Tomorrow? Need to steel myself for that.

29 January 1996

Exciting discovery today – a God of Silence! Harpocrates.

Lemprière: 'Harpocrates . . . supposed to be the same as Horus, son of Isis, among the Egyptians. He is represented as holding one of his fingers on his mouth, and hence he is called the god of silence and intimates that the mysteries of philosophy and religion ought never to be revealed to the people . . . placed by the Romans at the entrance to their temples.'

Maybe at the entrance to the theatres?

Should I build a shrine to him here? He is represented as a small boy – the child with his finger across his mouth. Imagine those eyes.

1 February 1996

'He carried out the gestures and by doing this he found faith': Pascal.

Sitting at the desk. Leafing through notes. Hoping to find faith.

18 February 1996

Yesterday and the day before I wrote an opening page; the writer arriving home. The process generated a soft flurry of excitement. But New York tomorrow for casting.[4] Escape!

16 May 1996

Tree men from Ballybofey are here to cut down 160 sitka spruce. 1,300 were planted behind the cottage in 1983. Last month one-third of the alder behind the house were cut down. The alder are stacked up opposite the courtyard.

23 May 1996

Put on a second super in the hive.

24 May 1996

The new dog, Molly, is here since last Tuesday, 21 May. The second dog, Daisy, is due tonight with David.

28 May 1996

Both dogs are thriving.

Trying – again – to work. Up early every morning and at the desk. So far to absolutely no avail.

7 June 1996

Still – and *so* reluctantly! – at the first three pages. And at each attempt the effort to prod it forward just by a line or two is almost too much and can so easily be quenched by indifference or the stuff's worthlessness or by complete disbelief in what is being attempted.

Got a swarm of bees in the walled garden close to Hive 1 and last night put it into Hive 2. Fed it (3 pints/3lbs) this morning.

12 June 1996

Rewrote the first six pages again yesterday for the hundredth time. I *think* the purpose of all those rewritings is to get the voice right. At this stage it is more important – well, at least as important – to get the pitch, tone, timbre right than to get *what* is said right. Maybe what is said can be said only in a certain voice. Or maybe what one says and how one says it constantly adjust one another.

All of which is a tactic to postpone tackling page 7.

24 June 1996

This morning I gathered together the notes and notebooks and pieces of paper and the first ten pages and put them into a cardboard box.

The act requires some courage. A formal acknowledgement of failure has to be made.

But the formal putting away of the stuff has two other elements. By banishing the material (what a dramatic word!) there is a sense of punishing it for disappointing me (and that is more than fleet-ingly righteous!). And at the back of the mind a suspicion that the material may sneak back, contrite, obedient, perhaps annealed. So in the act of banishing there is a feint [*sic*] cunning. (And the recognition of that cunning is pathetic, too!)

2 July 1996

A signal – weak, distant, but with some assurance – from the play this a.m. that perhaps I should return to it.

What can I do but respond?

I won't drop everything and plunge obediently in. But tomor-row I will call back, 'Yes?'

Meantime I took out the notes and notebooks and looked through them. Sirens.

What a flirtatious game!

30 September 1996

GIVE ME YOUR ANSWER, DO! was left with the typist last night.

Strange feeling of emptiness and disappointment and *tristesse*. But after *this* play surely I should be able to cope with the Neces-sary Uncertainty?

Seven Notes for a Festival Programme (1999)

1 Words

The tools that are available to the playwright to tell his story are
few enough – words, action, silence. In the theatre that has
engaged me words are at the very core of it all. The same words
that are available to the novelist, to the poet; and used with the
same precision and with the same scrupulous attention not only to
the exact kernel meaning but to all those allusive meanings that
every word hoards. But there is a difference. The playwright's
words aren't written for solitary engagement – they are written
for public utterance. They are used as the story-teller uses them, to
hold an audience in his embrace and within that vocal sound. So,
unlike the words of the novelist or poet, the playwright's words
are scored for a very different context. And for that reason they
are scored in altogether different keys and in altogether different
tempi. And it is with this score that the playwright and the actor
privately plot to work their public spell.

But even though these written words aren't fully empowered
until an actor liberates them and fulfils them, when that happens –
and if the playwright is in full mastery of his craft – then that
theatrical language acquires its own special joy and delight;
because what is written to be sung is now being sung. So that the
language in its meticulous use and in its accomplished utterance
finally and fully realizes itself. So that what the playwright wrote
– and even as he wrote listened closely to and actually heard – has
now been transferred to the stage, and those words, written in privacy and out of privacy but for public utterance, are now fulfilling
themselves completely. A private wisdom is being proclaimed
from the rooftops.

There is no contradiction in this. It is a contrived miracle – well,
a trick of the trade. Because the public utterance must still retain

that private intimacy where it has its origins. And even though the audience hears what it calls speeches, it hears too the author's private voice, that intimate language, that personal utterance. And that composite, that duet – the private and intimate set free into public canticle where both voices are distinctly audible – that is what makes the experience of theatre unique. And every time that happens the theatre fulfils itself again.

2 Great Actors

I have worked with many great actors over the years and the experience of working with them in the rehearsal room is one of the great joys and satisfactions of the theatre.

A great actor mustn't be confused with a star. He or she may be a star. But that isn't central to what he is, nor is it something he aspires to. What is it then that makes an actor great? And for convenience I'll refer to him as he.

First of all, his theatrical instincts are so finally tuned that he moves into those plays that offer his particular physical and intellectual capacities their full reach. And he makes those choices mostly intuitively. So that the plays he chooses to do challenge him but they also affirm him.

When he reads a play, in a sense he reads it with his ears. And what he sees on the page isn't necessarily the character so carefully described by the author but a version of himself, himself assuming those characteristics and making them his characteristics; sees himself penetrating that character and being suffused by it; so that what will finally emerge will be neither quite what the author wrote, nor what the actor is, but a new identity that draws from the essences of both. That is why we call it 'creating a part'.

But there is another way in which great actors manifest themselves: they are wonderful singers of the written line – perfect pitch, perfect rhythm. And they can do that because they know intuitively the exact meaning of that line; and not only the exact meaning but how that line was composed and why those words and only those words were used. So that not only does he understand the precise composition of a line but he knows that this line is inevitable now because of what was said in the preceding line; and the line that follows will be inevitable because of what is said now. So each of these lines, following necessarily on one another, generates the necessary propulsion of the text. And the great actor knows all that – intuitively. So that once he understands the engine of the play he can transform the text into an opera that is indeed greater than the writing and greater than its enactment. That is why great actors are scrupulous with the text. That is why great actors don't improvise. And that is why writers owe so much to them. We aren't mute any more.

They bestow eloquence on us.

3 Amateurs

One of the vigours of our theatre has been its roots in the amateur movement. Yeats acknowledged that vigour and tapped into its untutored energy. Indeed, the Abbey Theatre used that source until the sixties; and it nurtured the uncertain institution satisfactorily.

What did the amateur movement offer? It offered energy – mental energy, physical energy. It supplied a quick and intuitive imagination. It brought to the theatre a great enthusiasm and an eagerness to show off. 'Come and look at us because we have a natural talent for performance and it's all going to be the best of fun and it gives ourselves and our friends a great laugh.' And indeed all this was a useful antidote to the vanity and self-regard of the gathering of fifty in the drawing-room and their starchy hostess.[1]

But the days of the amateur having anything to contribute to the theatre are long gone. Because over the years the theatre, like every profession, has become more and more specialized. The amateur's high spirits are now applauded only in the parish hall. Because now we want our actors to have the finely tuned bodies of athletes. We insist that they have the same control over their breathing and their voices as the trained singer. We ask that they can dance and ride horses and swim and fence and speak a couple of languages – as well, of course, as being able to analyse a text closely and then interpret it with consummate skill.

And do we have these magnificent creatures? I think they are beginning to emerge. There is still a residue of the amateur traces in our theatre today – groups who had fun putting on plays when they were in college and who stayed together and worked together after college. But the brio and high spirits of the old days are no substitute for training. And today that training is vital. But we have efficient drama courses being taught all over the country. And more and more highly trained actors are available. And I now believe that a great theatre – which is possible only with great actors – is more and more possible here. If these great actors aren't seduced into film – which they will be if we don't recompense them adequately. But that's another story.

4 Music

I have used a lot of music in the plays over the years – nocturnes, jazz, symphonies, *céilí* bands, piano accordion.

In some ways the music I chose was in part a gesture to people I loved. For example, I used Tom Moore's 'Oft in the Stilly Night' in two plays[2] because sixty years ago my father taught that song to his school choir which I was in, and we won the cup at Omagh Feis and he was inordinately proud of us – and of himself. And for months afterwards he would line us up and start us off singing that Moore song. Then he would leave the classroom and cross the school yard and go to the far side of the country road and just stand there – listening to us singing in harmony in the distance. And although I couldn't see him standing there, I knew that we transported him. And I imagine that that may have been my earliest intimation of the power of music to move an audience.

In a play called *Give Me Your Answer, Do!* I used Mendelssohn's 'On Wings of a Song' because my two sisters sang that duet when they were about nine or ten. And even though the piece is clichéd I suppose it evokes for me a time of simpler pleasures and imagined innocence. So that even now I hear their voices, wavering and uncertain, 'On wings of a song I'll wander / With thee, my sister, I'll glide'. And I tell myself fancifully it is their unease before their difficult years ahead, just like the difficulties that confront Daisy in the play. But maybe these linkings between fact and fiction are too fanciful.

And I used a song called 'Down by the Cane-Break' in a play called *Wonderful Tennessee* because it was a song my mother sang; and because the words of the song – the promise of happiness in the Eden of Tennessee – those words echo the theme of the play.

And in *Philadelphia, Here I Come!* I used a piece of *céilí* music – or what one of the characters calls a 'piece of aul thumpety-thump'. And a similar piece – only more anguished and manic – in *Dancing at Lughnasa*. And in both plays the purpose was to explode theatrically the stifling rituals and discretions of family life. And since words didn't seem to be up to the job it was necessary to supply the characters with a new language. Because at that specific point in both plays when the *céilí* music is used, words offer neither an adequate means of expression nor a valve for emotional release. Because at that specific point emotion has staggered into inarticulacy beyond the boundaries of language. And that is what music can provide in the theatre: another way of talking, a language without words. And because it is wordless it can hit straight and unmediated into the vein of deep emotion.

5 Directors

Over the years I have worked with dozens of directors and, with a few exceptions, they have been very agreeable to work with. Why is it then that I have never quite come to terms with the idea of a director? I think it must be because after all these years I'm still not at all sure what this person contributes. For 2,500 years, since the time of Aeschylus, there was no such thing as a theatre director. And then they appear – suddenly – about 150 years ago and infiltrate the process and make themselves central to the making of theatre; so central that the production of a play today without a director is unthinkable. But let's look at this again. Why is the entire putting together of a play – choosing the actors, set designer, lighting designer, costume designer, understanding the text, realizing that text – why are all these responsibilities entrusted to one man or woman who has no training whatever in any of these jobs, who can't design sets, who can't write plays, who can't act? – although he or she probably tried to be an actor once. Why? And why do actors place themselves so docilely in the hands of this person? And why is the playwright asked to entrust the realization of his play in the hands of this interloper who has no demonstrable skills?

And how they crept into the process is not at all clear. Probably by accident. Just as we once thought that a bus must have a conductor. Until one day we realized that the conductor was altogether superfluous. Of course directors are convenient. Actor-managers who used to do the job could now concentrate on acting or managing. Theatrical producers who may be juggling four or five plays at the same time were happy to hand over some of that burden to the director, who would carry out his subcontract obediently. Actors weren't unhappy: here was an authoritative figure who makes sure that rehearsals are structured and the play is put together in a workman-like way. And more importantly from the actors' point of view, isn't the whole process being overseen by somebody who – out of all the actors available – chose me? So mustn't he or she be a very perceptive person? Who wouldn't want to trust that person, to serve that person?

But none of this tells us what the director does. Efficient management of a process. Yes, that's useful; but scarcely enough, is it? A unique interpretation of the text? I have never experienced that. A rare gift to draw out the full creative potential of the actors? I've never seen that either. So I'm puzzled. But what I do know about directors is this – because I have witnessed it: that the creativity and intelligence of actors, even great actors, can be sapped by placing their talents unquestioningly into those hands. And what I know, too – because I have witnessed it – is that directors attempt to usurp the intrinsic power of the play itself. Of course they insist their role is to serve the text, to ensure the play is given space and air to sing out. But in their hearts the song they want heard is their song because this is their interpretation, this is their vision. It is a sorry pass.

Of course, there have been a handful of magnificent directors in the short time of their existence – people like Stanislavsky, Guthrie, Grotowski, Brook. But their talent lay not in offering personal interpretation of a text but in exploding a whole calcified tradition, in turning upside down the whole practice of theatrical presentation so that we saw it all anew. They didn't offer us deep personal revelations but an entirely new kind of experience in the theatre. But innovators like that come around all too seldom. So let's not wait. And let's not be bamboozled by the bus conductors. I'll happily settle for a stage manager – if he can manage competently, and especially if he or she never wanted to be an actor.

6 Translations

I have done four translations from the Russian – Chekhov's *Three Sisters* and *Uncle Vanya*, and two versions of Turgenev, his play *A Month in the Country* and a stage version of his novel, *Fathers and Sons*. And over the years I have circled around Gorky and Gogol and Ostrovsky but for some reason haven't attempted them.

I'm not sure why I find the late-nineteenth-century Russians so sympathetic. Maybe because the characters in the plays behave as if their old certainties were as sustaining as ever – even though they know in their hearts that their society is in melt-down and the future has neither a welcome nor even an accommodation for them. Maybe a bit like people of my own generation in Ireland today. Or maybe I find those Russians sympathetic because they have no expectations whatever from love but still invest everything in it. Or maybe they attract me because they seem to expect that their problems will disappear if they talk about them – endlessly.

Anyhow, when I looked closely at these texts the experience of those people seemed very much at odds with the experience as offered in most of the English translations. For example, the received wisdom was that Chekhov was wistful and elusive and sweetly melancholy; and the English translations of the past sixty years have compounded that misreading. And the received wisdom was that Turgenev was a dilettante caught between his Slavophile and his Europhile leanings and finally was faithful to neither.

I think these readings are unfaithful to both men. But then the notion of faithfulness – of fidelity – to an original text is a complex one. How possible is translation at all? I have written myself about being faithful to the spirit of a text.[3] But now I'm not at all sure I know what that means. Borges has elegantly turned the whole notion on its head. He says originals have a way of being unfaithful to their translation – and in his heart every translator knows the truth of that. On the other hand Nabokov has said that a translation should read like a translation and should keep reminding the reader of its artificiality; it must insist, 'this is counterfeit'. I find this difficult. The various disbeliefs that the theatre asks us to suspend cannot be added to by demanding that we keep acknowledging that we are watching a counterfeit. Because we know that already; and the moment the curtain goes up we agree to enter into a make-believe and connive with it.

But maybe the pleasure I got from doing those four Russian plays had to do with the actors I had in all four. *Three Sisters* was an early Field Day production in the days when we were brash with assurance. *A Month in the Country* and *Vanya* were done beautifully at The Gate. And *Fathers and Sons* in the National Theatre in London with a cast that was collectively thrilling. And with actors like those I had in Derry, Dublin and in London any half-decent translation must be exciting.

7 Kitezh

There is a Russian folk-tale about a mythical town called Kitezh.[4]

The story goes that when Kitezh sensed that marauders were approaching, it encased itself in a mist and shrank into it and vanished from sight. But even as it disappeared, even after it had disappeared, the church bell never stopped ringing and could be heard through the mist and over the whole countryside.

I suppose like all folk-tales this story can be interpreted in whatever way your needs require. But for me the true gift of theatre, the real benediction of all art, is the ringing bell which reverberates quietly and persistently in the head long after the curtain has come down and the audience has gone home. Because until the marauders withdraw and the fog lifts, that sacred song is the only momentary stay we have against confusion.

Notes

In Interview with Graham Morison (1965)

1. Consciously or otherwise, Friel here echoes Yeats's notion of 'emotion of multitude'. See W. B. Yeats, *Essays and Introductions* (London: Macmillan, 1961), pp. 215–16.
2. Perhaps Friel is here thinking of Behan's comments on *The Hostage*. Behan argued in support of the director Joan Littlewood's use of Brechtian techniques as against Frank Dermody's, who directed *An Giall* in Dublin in June 1958. 'He [Dermody]'s of the school of Abbey Theatre naturalism of which I'm not a pupil. Joan Littlewood, I found, suited my requirements exactly . . . I've always thought T. S. Eliot wasn't far wrong when he said that the main problem today was to keep his audience amused; and that while they were laughing their heads off, you could be up to any bloody thing behind their backs; and that it was what you were doing behind their bloody backs that made your play great.' Brendan Behan, *Brendan Behan's Island: An Irish Sketch-book* (London: Hutchinson, 1962), p. 17.
3. The Ulster Group Theatre's failure to stage Sam Thompson's *Over the Bridge* (1960) hastened its collapse. See Sam Hanna Bell, *The Theatre in Ulster* (Dublin: Gill and Macmillan, 1972), p. 92.

The Theatre of Hope and Despair (1967)

1. Robert Brustein, *The Theatre of Revolt: An Approach to the Modern Drama* (Boston: Little, Brown, 1964), p. 10.
2. Harold Pinter, *The Dumb Waiter* (1960).
3. Jean Genet, *The Balcony* (1957).
4. Peter Weiss, *Marat/Sade* (1964).
5. Jack Gelber, *The Connection* (1959).
6. Either Edward Albee, *A Delicate Balance* (1964) or Friedrich Dürenmatt, *The Fireraisers* (1958).
7. Joe Orton, *Entertaining Mr Sloane* (1964).
8. Rolf Hochhuth, *The Deputy* (1963).
9. Possibly Frank Marcus, *The Killing of Sister George* (1966).
10. Charles Dyer, *Staircase* (1966).
11. Abe Burrows, *Cactus Flower* (1964), a Broadway musical.
12. Albert Camus, *The Rebel: An Essay on Man in Revolt*, trans. Anthony Bower (London: Penguin/Hamish Hamilton, 1971), p. 269.

In Interview with Desmond Rushe (1970)

1. This would have been the story 'The Child', in *The Bell,* 18.4 (July 1952), 232–33.
2. 'The Skelper', *The New Yorker,* 15 August 1959.
3. Friel had already written one farce, *The Mundy Scheme* (1969), and was to write another many years later, *The Communication Cord* (1982).
4. Cf. W. B. Yeats, citing Hugo, 'It is in the Theatre that the mob becomes a people.' *Uncollected Prose by W. B. Yeats*, ed. John P. Frayne and Colton Johnson, 2 (London: Macmillan, 1975), p. 286.

In Interview with Des Hickey and Gus Smith (1972)

1. Lady Gregory, *Our Irish Theatre* (Gerrards Cross: Colin Smythe, 1972), p. 131.
2. *The Mundy Scheme* was first staged at the Olympia Theatre, Dublin, on 10 June 1969, directed by Donal Donnelly and with Godfrey Quigley as F. X. Ryan.

Self Portrait (1972)

1. See, for example, Seamus Heaney, 'Feeling into Words', in *Preoccupations: Selected Prose 1968–1978* (London and Boston: Faber and Faber, 1980), pp. 47–8.

Plays Peasant and Unpeasant (1972)

1. W. B. Yeats, 'A People's Theatre', *Explorations* (London: Macmillan, 1962), pp. 254, 250.
2. *A State of Chassis*, by Tomás MacAnna and John D. Stewart, Peacock Theatre, 16 September 1970.
3. Sean O'Faolain, *The Irish* (Harmondsworth: Penguin, 1947, revised 1969), pp. 143–44.
4. This passage carries an echo of T. S. Eliot's essay, 'Tradition and the Individual Talent', in *Selected Prose of T. S. Eliot,* ed. Frank Kermode (London: Faber and Faber, 1975), pp. 37–44 (p. 41).
5. Ibid.
6. The reference is to the Irish Theatre Company, actually established in 1974 and dissolved by the Arts Council in 1982.

In Interview with Eavan Boland (1973)

1. For 'Foundry House', see Brian Friel, *The Saucer of Larks* (1962).
2. See T. S. Eliot, 'Tradition and the Individual Talent', in *Selected Prose of T. S. Eliot,* ed. Frank Kermode (London: Faber and Faber, 1975), p. 41.
3. It was *The Mundy Scheme* (1969) which was rejected by The Abbey.

Extracts from a Sporadic Diary (1976–78)

1. Eugene O'Neill to George Jean Nathan, 13 May 1939, concerning O'Casey's *The Star Turns Red* (1940). See *Selected Letters of Eugene O'Neill*, ed. Travis Bogard and Jackson R. Bryer (New Haven: Yale University Press, 1988), p. 486.

In Interview with Elgy Gillespie (1978)

1. See T. S. Eliot, 'The Possibility of a Poetic Drama', in *The Sacred Wood* (London: Faber and Faber, 1997), p. 50.
2. Ibid., p. 57.

Extracts from a Sporadic Diary (1979): *Translations*

1. Colonel Thomas Colby, *Ordnance Survey of the County of Londonderry: Memoir of the City and North Western Liberties of Londonderry*, Parish of Templemore (Dublin: Hodges, 1837).
2. J. H. Andrews, *A Paper Landscape: The Ordnance Survey in Nineteenth Century Ireland* (Oxford: Clarendon Press, 1975).
3. P. J. Dowling, *The Hedge Schools of Ireland* (Cork: Mercier Press, 1968 [1935]).
4. George Steiner, *After Babel: Aspects of Language and Translation* (Oxford: Oxford University Press, 1975).

In Interview with Victoria Radin (1981)

1. In 1994, however, following the international success of *Dancing at Lughnasa*, London accorded belated accolades to *Philadelphia, Here I Come!*, which ran for many months in the West End.
2. Kenneth Tynan's review of *The Quare Fellow*, in the *Observer*, 27 May 1956. 'The English hoard words like misers; the Irish spend them like sailors; and in Brendan Behan's tremendous new play language is out on a spree, ribald, dauntless and spoiling for a fight.'
3. Walter Kerr, '"Faith Healer" – A Play that Risks All', *New York Times*, 15 April 1979, D, pp. 3, 9.

In Interview with Fintan O'Toole (1982)

1. This changed in 1986 when playwright Thomas Kilroy, a Southerner, was added to the Board.
2. Kenneth Tynan, 'The End of the Noose' [review of Brendan Behan's *The Quare Fellow*], in the *Observer*, 27 May 1956, p. 11. See above, n. 2.
3. *The Philadelphia Story* (1939), an American play by Philip Barry, was filmed with Katharine Hepburn in the leading role and was later adapted as the musical film *High Society* (1956), starring Grace Kelly.
4. The reference is to Yeats's one-act play *Cathleen Ni Houlihan* (1902), which in later years Yeats feared may have acted as propaganda to inspire the 1916 Rising. See Yeats's poem 'The Man and the Echo', in *Collected Poems* (London: Macmillan, 1950), p. 393.

5. Gaelic Athletic Association, founded in 1884 and often associated with extreme nationalism. (Cf. Joyce's parody of the founder Michael Cusack as the Citizen in *Ulysses*.)

Making a Reply to the Criticisms of *Translations* by J. H. Andrews (1983)

1. J. H. Andrews had pointed out that the sappers did not carry bayonets. 'Before soldiers went on Survey duty they had to hand in their bayonets. Confronted with crime or civil disturbance, what Captain Lancey would really have done was withdraw and leave everything to the local constabulary.' *Crane Bag*, 7.2 (1983), 120.
2. Not to be outdone, J. H. Andrews later supplied even more examples of what he regarded as liberties with historical accuracy. See his 'Notes for a Future Edition of Brian Friel's *Translations*', *Irish Review*, 13 (1992–93), 93–106.

Programme Note for *Making History* (1988)

1. It is difficult not to believe that here Friel was responding to criticism made of the historical details of *Translations*. See his reply to J. H. Andrews above, p. 112.

Preface to *The London Vertigo* (1990)

1. Friel here quotes from his own version (p. 26). The original text is somewhat different. See *Four Comedies by Charles Macklin*, ed. J. O. Bartley (London: Sidgwick and Jackson, 1968), pp. 94–5.
2. *The London Vertigo* was first staged by Gate Theatre Productions at Andrews Lane Theatre, Dublin, on 23 January 1992, directed by Judy Friel.

In Interview with Mel Gussow (1991)

1. See page 136 above.

Extracts from a Sporadic Diary (1992–94): *Molly Sweeney*

1. Nikolai Gogol, *The Inspector General* (1836). Friel's typescript actually gives the title as *The Inspector Calls*, a slip over J. B. Priestley's *An Inspector Calls* (1946).
2. Wallace Stevens, 'Thirteen Ways of Looking at a Blackbird', stanza V, *Selected Poems* (London: Faber and Faber, 1965), p. 44.
3. A clear indication that Friel had been reading Oliver Sacks's essay, 'To See and Not See', *The New Yorker*, LXIX.12 (10 May 1993), pp. 59–73.
4. Wallace Stevens, 'Sunday Morning', stanza IV, *Selected Poems*, p. 32.
5. T. S. Eliot, 'Dry Salvages', stanza V, *Four Quartets*, in *The Complete Poems and Plays 1909–1950* (New York: Harcourt, Brace and World, 1962), p. 136.

Extracts from a Sporadic Diary (1995–96): *Give Me Your Answer, Do!*

1. *Give Me Your Answer, Do!* was first staged at the Abbey Theatre on 12 March

1997, directed by Brian Friel. The text was published to coincide with the open-ing. A new production was staged at the Hampstead Theatre, London, on 30 March 1998, directed by Robin Lefevre.

2. See Ludwig Wittgenstein, *Tractatus Logico-Philosophicus*, trans. D. F. Pears and B. F. McGuinness, with introduction by Bertrand Russell (London: Rout-ledge and Kegan Paul, 1963).

3. Anna Akhmatova, *Way of All the Earth*, ed. D. M. Thomas (London: Secker and Warburg, 1979), p. 66, p. 93 n.

4. *Molly Sweeney* opened at the Criterion Center Laura Pels Theatre, New York, in March 1996, in a production by the Roundabout Theatre Company in asso-ciation with the Gate Theatre, Dublin, and Emanuel Azenberg. The cast was: Jason Robards (Mr Rice), Catherine Byrne (Molly Sweeney), Alfred Molina (Frank Sweeney).

Seven Notes for a Festival Programme (1999)

1. The reference seems to be to W. B. Yeats's ideas for the staging of *At the Hawk's Well* (1916). In 'Certain Noble Plays of Japan', written to coincide with the first production of this play in Lady Cunard's drawing room in London, Yeats called for an audience of only 'forty or fifty'. See his *Essays and Introduc-tions* (London: Macmillan, 1961), p. 221.

2. See *The Loves of Cass McGuire* (Dublin: Gallery Press, 1984), p. 64, and *Molly Sweeney* (Loughcrew, Oldcastle: Gallery Press, 1994), p. 31.

3. See Friel's preface to *A Month in the Country* (1992) above, p. 146. Compare his preface to *The London Vertigo* (1990) above, p. 134.

4. See above, p. 163.

Bibliography

A.(i) **The Short Stories of Brian Friel**

The Saucer of Larks. New York: Doubleday; London: Victor Gollancz, 1962
The Gold in the Sea. New York: Doubleday; London: Victor Gollancz, 1966

A. (ii) **The Plays of Brian Friel**

Dates in parentheses after the title refer to first production

The Enemy Within (1962). Dublin: Gallery Press, 1979
Philadelphia, Here I Come! (1964). London: Faber and Faber, 1965; New York: Farrar Straus, 1966
The Loves of Cass McGuire (1966). London: Faber and Faber, 1967; New York: Farrar Straus, 1967; Loughcrew, Oldcastle: Gallery Press, 1984
Lovers [Winners/Losers] (1967). New York: Farrar Straus, 1968; London: Faber and Faber, 1969; Loughcrew, Oldcastle: Gallery Press, 1984
Crystal and Fox (1968). London: Faber and Faber, 1970; Dublin: Gallery Press, 1984
The Mundy Scheme (1969). New York: Samuel French, 1970
The Gentle Island (1971). London: Davis-Poynter, 1973; Loughcrew, Oldcastle: Gallery Press, 1993
The Freedom of the City (1973). London: Faber and Faber, 1974; New York: Samuel French, 1979; Loughcrew, Oldcastle: Gallery Press, 1992
Volunteers (1975). London: Faber and Faber, 1979; Loughcrew, Oldcastle: Gallery Press, 1989
Living Quarters (1977). London: Faber and Faber, 1978; Loughcrew, Oldcastle: Gallery Press, 1992
Aristocrats (1979). Dublin: Gallery Press, 1980
Faith Healer (1979). London: Faber and Faber, 1980; Loughcrew, Oldcastle: Gallery Press, 1991
Translations (1980). London: Faber and Faber, 1981
American Welcome (1980). In *The Best Short Plays of 1981*, ed. Stanley Richards. Radnor, PA: Chilton Book Co., 1981
Anton Chekhov's 'Three Sisters': A Translation (1981). Dublin: Gallery Press, 1981
The Communication Cord (1982). London: Faber and Faber, 1983
Selected Plays (Philadelphia, Here I Come!, The Freedom of the City, Living Quarters, Aristocrats, Faith Healer, Translations), introduced by Seamus Deane. London: Faber and Faber, 1984, repr. as *Plays 1* 1998; Washington, DC: Catholic University of America Press, 1986

Fathers and Sons: After the Novel by Ivan Turgenev (1986). London: Faber and Faber, 1987

Making History (1988). London: Faber and Faber, 1989

Dancing at Lughnasa (1990). London: Faber and Faber, 1990

The London Vertigo (1992). Loughcrew, Oldcastle: Gallery Press, 1990

A Month in the Country: After Turgenev (1992). Loughcrew, Oldcastle; Gallery Press, 1992

Wonderful Tennessee (1993). Loughcrew, Oldcastle: Gallery Press, 1993

Molly Sweeney (1994). Loughcrew, Oldcastle: Gallery Press, 1994; New York: Penguin, 1995

Give Me Your Answer, Do! (1997). Loughcrew, Oldcastle: Gallery Press, 1997

Uncle Vanya: A Version of the Play by Anton Chekhov (1998). Loughcrew, Oldcastle: Gallery Press, 1998

Plays 2 (*A Month in the Country, Making History, Dancing at Lughnasa, Wonderful Tennessee, Molly Sweeney*), introduced by Christopher Murray. London: Faber and Faber, 1999

B. Secondary Bibliography (Selected)

Achilles, Jochen. 'Intercultural Relations in Brian Friel's Works'. In *The Internationalism of Irish Literature and Drama*, ed. Joseph McMinn. Gerrards Cross: Colin Smythe, 1992, pp. 3–15

Andrews, Elmer. *The Art of Brian Friel: Neither Reality Nor Dreams*. New York: St Martin's Press, 1994; London: Macmillan, 1995

Andrews, J. H. 'Notes for a Future Edition of Brian Friel's *Translations*'. *Irish Review*, 13 (1992–93), 93–106

Bertha, Csilla. '"Island of Otherness": Images of Irishness in Brian Friel's *Wonderful Tennessee*'. *Hungarian Journal of English and American Studies: Irish Drama Issue*, ed. Csilla Bertha, 2.2 (1996), 129–42

Binnie, Eric. 'Brecht and Friel: Some Irish Parallels'. *Modern Drama*, 31.3 (1988), 365–70

Bort, Eberhard (editor). *The State of Play: Irish Theatre in the Nineties*. Trier: Wissenschaftlicher Verlag Trier, 1996

Burke, Patrick. 'Field Day's Fables of Identity'. In *Perspectives of Irish Drama and Theatre*, ed. Jacqueline Genet and Richard Allen Cave. Gerrards Cross: Colin Smythe, 1991, pp. 140–44

'"As if Language No Longer Existed": Non-verbal Theatricality in the Plays of Friel'. In *Brian Friel: A Casebook*, ed. William Kerwin. New York: Garland, 1997, pp. 13–22

Dantanus, Ulf. *Brian Friel: A Study*. London: Faber and Faber, 1988

Deane, Seamus. *Celtic Revivals: Essays in Modern Irish Literature 1880–1980*. London: Faber and Faber, 1985, ch. 13

Etherton, Michael. *Contemporary Irish Dramatists*. London: Macmillan, 1989, ch. 4

FitzGibbon, Gerald. 'Garnering the Facts: Unreliable Narrators in Some Plays of Brian Friel'. In *Critical Approaches to Anglo-Irish Literature*, ed. Michael Allen and Angela Wilcox. Gerrards Cross: Colin Smythe, 1989, pp. 53–62

Guthrie, Tyrone. *In Various Directions: A View of the Theatre*. London: Michael Joseph, 1965

Hawkins, Maureen S. G. 'Schizophrenia and the Politics of Experience in Three Plays by Brian Friel'. *Modern Drama*, 39.3 (1996), 465–74

Huber, Werner. 'Irish vs. English: Brian Friel's *Making History*'. *Anglistik & Englischunterricht*, 41 (1990), 165–75

Jent, William. 'Immaterial Contingencies: Relativizing the Rage for the Absolute in Brian Friel's *Wonderful Tennessee*'. *Canadian Journal of Irish Studies*, 21.1 (July 1995), 25–44

Kearney, Richard. 'Language Play: Brian Friel and Ireland's Verbal Theatre'. *Studies*, 72 (spring 1985), 20–56

Kerwin, William (editor). *Brian Friel: A Casebook*. New York: Garland, 1997

Kiberd, Declan. *Inventing Ireland*. London: Jonathan Cape; Cambridge, MA: Harvard University Press, 1995, chs. 33, 34

Kosok, Heinz. 'Words *versus* Action in the Plays of Brian Friel'. *Plays and Playwrights from Ireland in International Perspective*. Trier: Wissenschaftlicher Verlag Trier, 1995, pp. 247–56

Krause, David. 'The Failed Words of Brian Friel'. *Modern Drama*, 40 (1997), 359–73

Kurdi, Mária. 'Rewriting the Reread: Brian Friel's Version of Turgenev's *A Month in the Country*'. *Irish University Review*, 25 (1995), 284–97

Lanters, José. 'Violence and Sacrifice in Brian Friel's *The Gentle Island* and *Wonderful Tennessee*'. *Irish University Review*, 26 (1996), 163–76

Lojek, Helen. 'Brian Friel's Plays and George Steiner's Linguistics'. *Contemporary Literature*, 35.1 (1994), 83–99

McGrath, F. C. 'Irish Babel: Brian Friel's *Translations* and George Steiner's *After Babel*'. *Comparative Drama*, 23.1 (1989), 31–49

    'Brian Friel and the Politics of Anglo-Irish Literature', *Colby Quarterly*, 26.4 (1990), 241–48

Mesterházi, Márton. 'A Practitioner's View of Brian Friel's *Wonderful Tennessee*', *Hungarian Journal of English and American Studies* 2.2 (1996), 143–53

Maxwell, D. E. S. *Brian Friel*. Lewisburg: Bucknell University Press, 1973

Meissner, Collin. 'Words between Worlds: The Irish Language, the English Army, and the Violence of Translation in Brian Friel's *Translations*'. *Colby Quarterly*, 28.3 (1992), 164–73

Murray, Christopher. 'Brian Friel's *Making History* and the Problem of Historical Accuracy'. In *The Crows behind the Plough: History and Violence in Anglo-Irish Poetry and Drama*, ed. Geert Lernout. Amsterdam: Rodopi, 1991, pp. 61–77

    'Friel's "Emblems of Adversity" and the Yeatsian Example'. In *The Achievement of Brian Friel*, ed. Alan J. Peacock. Gerrards Cross: Colin Smythe, 1993, pp. 69–90

    '"Recording Tremors": *Dancing at Lughnasa* and the Concept of Tradition'. In *Brian Friel: A Casebook*, ed. William Kerwin. New York: Garland, 1997, pp. 23–41

    Twentieth-Century Irish Drama: Mirror up to Nation. Manchester: Manchester University Press, 1997

'Brian Friel's *Molly Sweeney* and its Sources: A Postmodern Case History', *Études Irlandaises*, 23.2 (autumn 1998), 81–98

O'Brien, George. *Brian Friel*. Dublin: Gill and Macmillan, 1979; Boston: Twayne, 1980

　　Brian Friel: A Reference Guide 1962–1992. New York; G. K. Hall, 1995

O'Connor, Ulick. *Brian Friel: Crisis and Commitment. The Writer and Northern Ireland* [pamphlet]. Dublin: Elo Press, 1989

O'Toole, Fintan. 'Marking Time: From *Making History* to *Dancing at Lughnasa*'. In *The Achievement of Brian Friel*, ed. Alan J. Peacock. Gerrards Cross: Colin Smythe, 1993, pp. 202–14

Peacock, Alan J. (editor). *The Achievement of Brian Friel*. Gerrards Cross: Colin Smythe, 1993

Peacock, Alan J. and Kathleen Devine. '"In Touch with Some Otherness": The Double Vision of Brian Friel's *Dancing at Lughnasa*'. *Études Irlandaises*, 17.1 (June 1992), 113–127

　　'Other Dimensions: Myth, Ritual and Sacrifice in Brian Friel's *Wonderful Tennessee*'. *Études Irlandaises*, 22.1 (spring 1997), 85–100

Pelletier, Martine. 'Telling Stories and Making History: Brian Friel and Field Day'. *Irish University Review*, 24 (1994), 186–97

　　Le Théâtre de Brian Friel: histoire, histoires. Villeneuve d'Ascq: Presses Universitaires du Sepentrion, 1997

Pilkington, Lionel. 'Language and Politics in Brian Friel's *Translations*'. *Irish University Review*, 20 (1990), 282–98

Pine, Richard. *Brian Friel and Ireland's Drama*. London: Routledge, 1990; second edn. Dublin: UCD Press, 1999, under title *The Diviner: The Art of Brian Friel*

Richards, Shaun. 'Placed Identities for Placeless Times: Brian Friel and Post-Colonial Criticisim'. *Irish University Review*, 27 (1997), 55–68

Richtarik, Marilynn J. *Acting between the Lines: The Field Day Theatre Company and Irish Cultural Politics 1980–1984*. Oxford: Clarendon Press, 1994

Roche, Anthony. 'A Bit off the Map: Brian Friel's *Translations* and Shakespeare's *Henry IV*'. In *Literary Interrelations: Ireland, England, and the World*, ed. Wolfgang Zach and Heinz Kosok, vol. 2. Tübingen: Gunter Narr, 1987, pp. 139–48

　　Contemporary Irish Drama. Dublin: Gill and Macmillan, 1994

　　(editor) *Irish University Review: Special Issue: Brian Friel*, 29.1 (1999)

Schrank, Bernice. 'Politics and Language in the Plays of Sean O'Casey and Brian Friel'. In *Anglo-Irish and Irish Literature: Aspects of Language and Culture*, ed. Birgit Bramsbäck and Martin Croghan. 2 vols., Uppsala: University of Uppsala, 1988. Vol. 2, pp. 71–6

Smith, Robert S. 'The Hermeneutic Motion in Brian Friel's *Translations*.' *Modern Drama*, 34 (1991), 392–409

Steiner, George. *After Babel: Aspects of Language and Translation*. Oxford: Oxford University Press, 1975

Velten, Christa, '"Be faithful to the routine gestures and the bigger thing will come to you": Old Themes in Fermentation in Brian Friel's *Give Me Your Answer, Do!*' Unpublished paper delivered at IASIL conference, Limerick University, July 1998

White, Harry. 'Brian Friel, Thomas Murphy and the Use of Music in Contemporary Irish Drama'. *Modern Drama*, 33.4 (1990), 553–62

Wiley, Catherine. 'Recreating Ballybeg: Two Translations by Brian Friel'. *Journal of Dramatic Theory and Criticism*, 1.2 (1987), 51–61

Winkler, Elizabeth Hale. 'Brian Friel's *The Freedom of the City*: Historical Actuality and Dramatic Imagination'. *Canadian Journal of Irish Studies*, 7.1 (1981), 12–31

Worth, Katharine. 'Translations of History: Story-Telling in Brian Friel's Theatre'. In *British and Irish Drama since 1960*, ed. James Acheson. London: Macmillan, 1993, pp. 73–87

Worthen, W. B. 'Homeless Words: Field Day and the Politics of Translation'. *Modern Drama*, 38 (1995), 22–41

Zach, Wolfgang. 'Criticism, Theatre and Politics: Brian Friel's *The Freedom of the City* and its Early Reception'. In *Irish Literature and Culture*, ed. Michael Kenneally. Gerrards Cross: Colin Smythe, 1992, pp. 112–26

Acknowledgements

Acknowledgement is hereby made to all the original publishers of these pieces, whose courtesy is acknowledged.

'Playwright of the Western World' interview with Peter Lennon, 8 October 1964. © 1964, *Guardian*

'Interview with Graham Morison, 1965'. 'An Ulster Writer: Brian Friel', *Acorn*, 8 (Spring 1965) pp. 4–15. © University of Ulster, Magee College.

'The Theatre of Hope and Despair, 1967', *Everyman* 1 (1968), 17–22, Servite Publications. 'The author of *Philadelphia, Here I Come!* and *The Loves of Cass McGuire* talks about contemporary trends in his own art. First delivered as a lecture at the Thomas More Association Symposium, Chicago, and reprinted from "The Critic" by kind permission.'

'Interview with Desmond Rushe, 1970'. First published in *The Word*, February 1970, pp. 12–15, as 'Kathleen Mavourneen, Here Comes Brian Friel'. Reprinted with permission.

'In Discussion with Fergus Linehan, Hugh Leonard and John B. Keane, 1970'. First published in the *Irish Times* as 'The Future of Irish Drama', 12 July 1970. Reproduced with permission from the *Irish Times*.

'Self-Portrait, 1972', first published in *Aquarius*, 5 (1972), 17–22, Servite Publications. First given as a talk on BBC radio and printed by kind permission of producer John Boyd.

'In Interview with Des Hickey and Gus Smith, 1972'. 'Two Playwrights with a Single Theme', in *A Paler Shade of Green*, by Des Hickey and Gus Smith (London: Leslie Frewin, 1972). Reprinted by kind permission of Gus Smith.

'Plays Peasant and Unpeasant, 1972', *The Times Literary Supplement*, 17 March 1972, pp. 305-6. Reprinted by permission.

'Brian Friel: Derry's Playwright', interview with Eavan Boland, 16 February 1973 in *Hibernia*. © Hibernia National Review Ltd, Dir. John Mulcahy.

'Can the Critics Kill a Play' interview with Facthna O'Kelly, *Irish Press*, 28/29 March 1975, by permission of Irish Press plc.

'Extracts from a Sporadic Diary (1976–78)': *Aristocrats*. Reproduced with permission of The O'Brien Press, Dublin in *The Writers: A Sense of Ireland*, edited by Andrew Carpenter and Peter Fallon.

'Interview with Elgy Gillespie, 1978', 'Is the Play Still the Thing? – 4' *Irish Times*, 28 July 1978. Reproduced with permission from the *Irish Times*.

'Extracts from a Sporadic Diary, 1979', first published in *Ireland and the Arts*, ed. Tim Pat Coogan (London: Namara House n.d.)

'Interview with Ciaran Carty, 1980', first published as 'Finding Voice in a Language Not Our Own', an interview with Brian Friel by Ciaran Carty, first published in the *Sunday Independent*, Dublin, on 5 October 1980. Reprinted with permission, the editor, *Sunday Independent*.

'Interview with Paddy Agnew, 1980', was first published as 'Talking to Ourselves' by *Magill*, December 1980. Reproduced by permission of the holders of the *Magill* copyright for 1977 to October 1998.

'Programme Note for Tom Murphy's *The Blue Macushla*'. 'Exiles' programme, Abbey Theatre, March 1980. Reprinted by kind permission of the Abbey Theatre.

'Interview with Victoria Radin, 1981'. 'Voice from Ireland: Victoria Radin talks to Brian Friel', 1 March 1981. © 1981, *Observer*.

'Interview with Elgy Gillespie, 1981'. 'The Saturday Interview: Brian Friel', *Irish Times*, 'Weekend', 5 September 1981. Reproduced with permission from the *Irish Times*.

'Interview with Ray Comiskey, 1982'. 'Rehearsing Friel's New Farce'; *Irish Times*, 14 September 1982. Reproduced with permission from the *Irish Times*.

'Interview with Fintan O'Toole, 1982'. 'The Man from God Knows Where', *In Dublin*, 28 October 1982. Reproduced by kind permission of Fintan O'Toole.

'Making a Reply to the Criticism of *Translations* by J. H. Andrews, 1983'. From '*Translations* and *A Paper Landscape*: Between Fiction and History: Brian Friel, John Andrews and Kevin Barry', *The Crane Bag: The Forum Issue*, 7.2 (1983): 118–24. Reproduced by kind permission of the editors, *Crane Bag*.

'Important Places: A Preface', 1986. Introduction to Charles McGlinchey, *The Last of the Name* (Belfast: Blackstaff Press, 1986). Reproduced by permission of Blackstaff Press.

'Interview with Laurence Finnegan', M. Ed. Thesis, 1986, TCD, unpublished. By kind permission of Laurence Finnegan, the estate of Dr Daniel Murphy, and the Board of Trinity College.

'Programme Note for *Making History*, 1988'. (Field Day, Derry) September 1988. © Brian Friel. Reproduced by kind permission.

'Preface to *The London Vertigo*, 1990'. By kind permission of The Gallery Press. Loughcrew, Oldcastle, Gallery Press, 1990.

'Interview with Mel Gussow, 1991'. 'From Ballybeg to Broadway', by Mel Gussow, *New York Times Magazine*, 29 September 1991. © New York Times

'Preface to *A Month in the Country*, 1992'. Reproduced by kind permission of the

ACKNOWLEDGEMENTS

Gallery Press from Brian Friel, *A Month in the Country: After Turgenev*. Oldcastle, Loughcrew: Gallery Books, 1992

'Seven Notes for a Festival Programme, 1999'. Reproduced by kind permission of Mr Noel Pearson and Ferndale Theatre Productions.

Index

dedication to smash hits and long
runs, 22–3
Faith Healer, 94, 111, 144
Philadelphia, Here I Come!, xv, 4,
82, 92, 105
as a warehouse for theatrical mer-
chandise, 18, 48
Brook, Peter, 55, 178
Brustein, Robert, 20
Bulgakov, Mikhail Afanasievich, 154
Burke, Edmund, 137
Burke, Patrick, xv
Byrne, Catherine, 148
Byrne, Conal, 122
Byrne, Gay, 127

callisthenics, 14
Camus, Albert, 20, 24
Carleton, William, viii
Carroll, Paul Vincent, xv, 31
Carty, Ciaran, 79–83
Catholic emancipation, 116
céilí music, 177
Chekhov, Anton, 71, 92
accessibility, 67
and *Aristocrats*, xi, 99, 144
The Cherry Orchard, 150
F. often compared with, 141
misreading of, 179
The Seagull, 150, 152
Three Sisters, xi, 84, 95, 144, 179
and Turgenev, 152, 159
Uncle Vanya, 179
Chesterton, G. K., 66
Christian Brothers, 1, 128–9, 133
Church, the (Roman Catholic), xv, 20,
23, 25–6, 29, 52
Civil Rights Movement, 28, 48
Clarke, Austin, 54
Colby, Colonel, 74, 75, 117–18
colonialism, 116, 117
Columba, St, xiii, 2
Comiskey, Ray, 101–4
Communism, 21
Congreve, William, 93
The Countess Cathleen, 51
Covent Garden, London, 138
Croagh Patrick, 26
Cronyn, Hume, 144
Crow Street Theatre, Dublin, 137
Cuchulainn, 132

Dallas (television programme), 132

Dantanus, Ulf, vii, xv
Deane, Seamus, 94, 98, 105
Department of Education, 126
Derry, 59, 60, 145, 180
British army barracks, 83
Civil Rights demonstrations, 28
The Communication Cord staged in,
103
F. lives in, 1, 3, 26, 37, 82, 93, 105,
111, 143
F. teaches in, 1, 9, 37
Field Day's relationship with, 101–2
lack of other writers in, 47
no-man's-land in, 28
plans for a new theatre, 70, 98
Siege of, 87
Translations staged in, 79, 84–5, 98
unemployment, 79–80
Derry City Council, 79, 80, 82
Dickey, James: *Deliverance*, 57
Donegal, Co., 7, 28, 35, 47, 70, 105,
111, 116, 118, 136, 138, 145
Donnelly, Donal, 49
Doolan, Lelia, 52
Dostoievsky, Fyodor, 153–4
Dowling, Joe, 103, 140
Dowling, P. J.: *The Hedge Schools of
Ireland*, 74, 75, 116
'Down by the Cane-Break', 176–7
Down, Co., 137
Dublin, 35, 145, 180
demand for writing about permissive
Dublin, 53–4
F.'s feelings about, 31
F.'s plays launched in, 44
lack of a link with rural roots, 27
literary, 3, 14
and the new Ireland, 27
Post Office, 31
schizophrenia of, 54
theatrical tradition, 114
Dublin Arts Council, 82
Dublin Government, 28
Dublin Theatre Festival, 1, 94, 96, 103,
104
Dürrenmatt, Friedrich, 21, 90–91
Dynasty (television programme), 132

Edwards, Hilton, xiv, 3, 54
El Greco, 18
Eliot, T. S., xx, 53, 59, 70, 158
on Coleridge, 69
'Hamlet and his Problems', xvi